The Rustication of Urban Youth in China

THE
CHINA
BOOK
PROJECT Translation and Commentary

A wide-ranging series of carefully prepared translations of books published in China since 1949, each with an extended introduction by a Western scholar.

EDITED BY
PETER J. SEYBOLT

INTRODUCTION BY
THOMAS P. BERNSTEIN

The Rustication
of Urban Youth
in China A SOCIAL EXPERIMENT

M. E. SHARPE, INC., PUBLISHER, WHITE PLAINS, NEW YORK

Copyright © 1975, 1976, 1977 by M. E. Sharpe, Inc.
901 North Broadway, White Plains, New York 10603

Library of Congress Catalog Card Number: 76-17395
International Standard Book Number: 0-87332-082-4

Printed in the United States of America

From The China Book Project. The Rustication of Urban
Youth in China features a translation of Je-ch'ing kuan-huai
hsia-hsiang chih-shih ch'ing-nien ti ch'eng chang: Tso-hao
chih-shih ch'ing-nien shang-shan hsia-hsiang ti ching-yen
(Have a Warm Concern for the Growth of Educated Youths
Going down to the Countryside: The Experiences of Doing
a Good Job at the Work of Educated Youths Going up to the
Mountains and down to the Countryside) (Peking People's
Press, 1973). Translations of most of the material that
appears in this book were first published in the journal
Chinese Education.

Contents

Appendix

AOSSA

Preface

Peter J. Seybolt

This book is a compilation of documents dealing with one of the largest population movements and one of the most unusual social experiments in history. At a time when the population trend throughout the world is from rural to urban areas, China is seeking to reverse the process by sending millions of educated urban youths to the countryside to settle permanently.

In his introductory essay, Professor Thomas Bernstein discusses the history of the rural transfer movement, the reasons for it, the approximate numbers of people involved, and the problems that have been encountered.

The major source of this book is Have a Warm Concern for the Growth of Educated Youths Going down to the Countryside, which is translated here in full. Published in China in 1973 as part of an effort to reaffirm the policy of transferring urban youths to the countryside, it contains case studies which provide emulation models and guidelines for resolving problems. In an appendix we have included a number of other articles to illustrate additional aspects of the movement, such as problems relating to university admissions, love and marriage, and so on.

The English-language publication of these documents represents the work of a number of people. Chou Shan drafted the translation of the majority of the articles. Others were drafted by Perry Brainin, Ai Ping, and the editor, who was also responsible for selection of the materials and for checking and revising translations. I should like to thank the translators,

Thomas Bernstein for his introduction, and his help in the selection process, and Douglas Merwin of M. E. Sharpe, Inc., who participated in every aspect of the production of this book.

March 1977

Introduction

Thomas P. Bernstein

Definitions and Goals of the Program

The materials here reproduced deal with the transfer to the
countryside of young urbanites, youths born and raised in cities
and towns, and, for the most part, graduates of junior or senior
middle schools. Shang-shan hsia-hsiang, "up to the mountains
and down to the villages," as the transfer program is called,
must be distinguished from other flows of manpower from the
urban to the rural sector, such as the temporary or long-term
"sending down," hsia-fang, of cadres, or the dispatch to the
rural areas of doctors, scientists, or other specialized per-
sonnel. The program must also be distinguished from the return of peasants to their native villages upon completion of
schooling not available in their production teams or brigades.
The Chinese government has been promoting the return of educated peasant youths for many years, even before educated
young urbanites began to be sent to the countryside in large
numbers. Lumping the various categories together results in
erroneous assessments, for instance, of the developmental significance of these urban-to-rural flows. Thus, urban youths
usually do not possess highly specialized skills, whereas scientists and doctors obviously do. Similarly, lumping such
categories as the returned educated peasant youths (hui-hsiang
chih-shih ch'ing-nien) together with the urban sent-down educated youths (hsia-hsiang chih-shih ch'ing-nien) results in

xi

statistical confusion, since there are far more returned peasant youths than sent-down urban youths. Also, the problems
which returned educated peasants face are different from those
faced by young urbanites going to the villages. Other things
being equal, it is easier to readjust to one's native village than
to adapt to a wholly different environment. The Chinese press,
however, sometimes considers the returned and the sent-down
youths together, under the common label of "up to the mountains and down to the villages." Thus, a People's Daily editorial reprinted in this volume (pp. 3-8) speaks of sent-down
youths who grew up in the cities and had "seldom come into
contact with village society." But the editorial also singles
out as a model for emulation an educated youth named Hsing
Yen-tzu, who returned to her native village in 1958, eventually
rising to Central Committee membership, and concludes with
an appeal to "Young comrades going to the countryside and returning to the countryside." It is thus not always clear about
whom the press is writing, though in fact, most of the materials
in this volume do seem to deal with sent-down urban youth.

The transfer of urban youths began sometime in the mid-
1950s, but on a rather small scale. (1) It picked up momentum
after the Great Leap Forward, but even then the number of educated young urbanites sent to the countryside was small. According to an article published in December 1975 (pp. 168 ff),
only 1.2 million urban youths were sent to the villages in the
ten years preceding the Cultural Revolution, most in fact in
the years 1962-66. The transfer movement came into its own
in the wake of the Cultural Revolution. Between 1968 and the
end of 1975, 12 million urban youths were sent to the countryside. If it is assumed that the urban population consisted of
about 120 million inhabitants in the late 1960s, the transfer of
the 12 million would mean that about 10 percent of the urban
population has been removed from the urban sector under this
program. The rates of transfer have been quite uneven. In
the immediate post-Cultural Revolution years, 1968-1970, the
movement was intense, since about 5 or 6 million young people
were sent to the rural areas, mostly youths who had taken part

in the Red Guard movement. A slowdown occurred in the early 1970s, but in 1974 and 1975 the transfer again gained momentum, since in each of those years about 2 million young urbanites went "up to the mountains and down to the villages." In 1976, according to a report published late that year, the transfer was maintained at the high levels of 1974 and 1975. (2)

Urban youths have been sent to places both very far away and quite close to their hometowns. Some have been permitted to settle in suburban counties; others have gone to distant frontier provinces. Shanghai exemplifies this pattern: of the roughly 1 million youths sent since the Cultural Revolution, about 400,000 have settled in the ten suburban counties that are part of Shanghai Metropolis, while 600,000 have settled in such provinces as Anhwei and Kiangsi, but especially in far-distant Heilungkiang, Kirin, Inner Mongolia, Sinkiang, and Yunnan. However, only a few major cities, including Shanghai, Peking, Wuhan, Nanking, and Tientsin, account for the bulk of the interprovincial transfer. In most provinces, urban youths are sent to destinations within the home province, although the distances can vary widely also. Thus, youths from Canton may be sent to a nearby commune in such counties as Ssu-hui or Tseng-ch'eng, or to Hainan Island, which is quite far away. The impact of the transfer on individual youths can thus vary enormously. For example, a Shanghai youth who settles in a suburban commune can frequently visit relatives; one sent to Heilungkiang can do so at best once a year.

Urban youths settle on people's communes, state farms, or on farms operated by the PLA's Production and Construction Corps. Here too, there are considerable differences. On communes, for instance, they receive variable work points, in contrast to regular wages paid on state and army farms. Life on the latter, especially on the army farms, is more highly collectivized and discipline is stricter than on communes. PLA farms are also likely to be located in the frontier provinces, such as Heilungkiang, Inner Mongolia, and Sinkiang. A major purpose of the frontier settlement is not only to open up new land for settlement but to bolster the Han Chinese presence in highly sensitive areas, given the confrontation with the Soviet Union.

The transfer program differs from the American Peace Corps or from military service in that the stay in the rural areas is in principle permanent. The expectation that sent-down youths will strike roots (cha-ken) in the villages and stay for life (i-pei-tzu) is the most dramatically revolutionary element in this program. "Up to the mountains and down to the villages" aims at turning urbanites into peasants, at reversing the process normal for most modernizing countries, namely, of going from the villages to the cities. It is the principle of permanence that creates difficulties in the implementation of the program, necessitating extensive mobilization of organizational and ideological resources to secure compliance. The idea of urbanites taking up permanent residence in the rural areas runs counter to values to which a good many urbanites continue to adhere, such as that an urban-based career is more desirable and more rewarding than a rural-based one. (3) Such values, it is worth noting, are rooted in the existence of significant rural-urban inequalities, which persist even though efforts have been made to reduce them. The dramatic change in values which the transfer program demands is well expressed in this quote from a Red Flag article:

> Each educated youth must decide whether to strike true or false roots in the village. When educated youths go to the village, they must establish an attitude of persisting in the village for life, becoming revolutionaries with an iron resolve to serve the peasants (t'ieh-hsin wu-nung ti ko-ming che). They must decide that they will not just hurriedly pass through the village. To go down to the countryside for three years is rather easy; what is hard is to strike roots for life. (4)

Thus, if return were guaranteed, if the transfer program were a rotation system, the program would be far easier to implement. There is little doubt that in a service-oriented mobilization system such as China, urban youth would readily assum⌐

the burden of service in the rural areas, provided return were assured.

The for-life principle notwithstanding, policy has permitted a proportion of sent-down youths to return to the urban sector, either to take up factory work or to attend a higher educational institution. With regard to the former, some youths have been assigned every year to state-owned industrial enterprises, not necessarily in their hometowns, but also in the county towns of the area to which they had been sent. Whether assignment to a college or university entails departure from the rural sector is a controversial question since, in principle, graduates of higher schools are supposed to return to the units from which they came. Yet, in fact, it appears that for a substantial pro-portion of those chosen for higher study, the opportunity has in fact meant long-term return to the urban sector, i.e., to an ad-ministrative agency located in a city or town. (5) It is not clear just how many sent-down urban youths have been chosen to at-tend higher schools. The number cannot have been very large, since as of 1974 the student body in China's colleges and uni-versities totaled only about 400,000, at a time when 10 million urban youths were serving in the rural areas and also consider-ing that it is by no means only sent-down youths who are se-lected for higher study. Most of those reassigned to the urban sector have thus become factory workers, as the references to reassignment in this volume in fact suggest. A global statistic for return to the urban sector is not available. One uncon-firmed estimate is that as of 1973 one fourth of 8 million urban youths then in the villages had been reassigned. An example in this volume would suggest that the total has been even larger: in Huai-te county, Kirin, 607 youths had come from Shanghai and the county town since 1968. As of 1973, 345 were still there, a departure rate of 43 percent (p. 29). But this seems unusually large, and indications are that probably only a fairly small minority has been able to return to the urban sector. (6)

It would be remarkable if more than a minority had returned, for not only would this contradict the oft-repeated "for life" principle, but it would also put into question one of the fundamental reasons why the transfer program was adopted in the first place. The rustication program is rooted in the incapacity of the urban sector to supply enough jobs to all those entering the urban job market. Already in the 1950s, when industry grew at unprecedented rates, it had proven necessary to restrict peasant migration. By 1957, a problem had also arisen of providing employment for urban youths just graduating from school. Temporarily obscured by the opportunities created by the Great Leap Forward expansion, this problem resurfaced again in the 1960s and has existed ever since, accentuated by the high urban birthrates of the 1950s and early 1960s. (7)

Data relating urban employment rates to the transfer of urban youths, however, are virtually nonexistent. One indicator of the dimensions of the problem came to the surface during the Cultural Revolution, when a Red Guard tabloid quoted a planner as saying that in the Third Five-Year Plan, rescheduled to run from 1966 to 1970, 11 million persons would enter the urban job market from within, of whom only 5 million could be provided with jobs. (8) The remaining 6 million, it is worthy of note, roughly corresponds to the number actually sent to the countryside from 1968 to 1970, the transfer having in effect been suspended in 1966 and 1967. Although the mass transfer of Red Guards to the countryside has often been attributed to the need to restore order in the cities, and rightly so, the actual number sent to the villages appears to have been related to the capacity of the urban sector to provide young people with employment. For the 1970s qualitative data suggest the continued existence of a substantial though varying gap between the number of young people graduating from secondary school and the number that can be given urban jobs. Thus, in any one year, it is usually only a proportion of the graduating middle school class that is sent to the countryside.

The transfer program is motivated not only by considerations of urban employment. Two other goals sustain it, that of ideological transformation and that of speeding up rural development. Indeed, it is these two that are always mentioned in the press as the two essential goals of the program, as the materials in this volume amply confirm. With regard to ideological change, the program has been defined as an important component in the struggle against revisionism and for the consolidation of the dictatorship of the proletariat. The program is also seen as making a contribution to the ultimate goal of eliminating the "three great differences," those between town and country, manual and mental labor, worker and peasant. More specifically, the transfer movement aims at rearing "revolutionary successors," who will be motivated primarily by an ethic of unselfish service to the collective good rather than by selfish pursuit of comfortable and prestigious careers. As such it is part of the "revolution in education" that has been in progress since 1966 and which aims at fundamentally changing the motivations of young people who receive education. Under normal circumstances, education usually stimulates demand for more education and for entry into prestigious white-collar jobs, or as the press puts it, one studies to become an official, tu-shu tso-kuan. In secondary school, the aspirations to rise to the top express themselves in fierce competition to enter higher schools. Since the Cultural Revolution, however, the state has severed secondary education from the issue of entrance into colleges and universities by requiring that graduates spend at least two years in production before becoming eligible for higher education. Moreover, when students are chosen, it is their production record and the recommendation of their production units that is supposed to weigh heavily in the admissions decision, rather than performance in school. And, when students graduate from higher schools, they are supposed to return to the units whence they came, as already noted. Thus, the educational system's mission is to prepare "cultured" workers and peasants rather than elite-minded careerists. The transfer program is seen as a major means to attain this end. Sent-down youths are to be "reeducated" (tsai chiao-yü) by the poor and lower-middle peasants; it is hoped that sustained contact with the peasants will lead to thoroughgoing value change.

One of the anti-elitist goals of the revolution in education and of the transfer movement has been to eliminate status transmission in Chinese society, i.e., to end the capacity of high status parents to pass their advantages on to their offspring. In the case of children of the old upper classes, for instance, entrance to higher education has been virtually closed to them since the Cultural Revolution. What is remarkable is that a substantial effort has also been made to enforce this goal in the case of children of the current elite, whose parents occupy high positions in the political and military hierarchies. Thus, cases abound in the press of high-ranking cadres who insist on sending their children to the countryside, despite the opportunities which are open to them to secure preferential assignment for their offspring. The goal here is to avoid replication of the pattern characteristic of the "revisionist" socialist countries, in which a high proportion of students in prestige universities come from elite parents. In this volume, several chapters depict high-ranking cadres as taking the lead in sending their children to the countryside, asking them, as it were, to start again from the bottom. In one case, such a youth ends up marrying a peasant (see Chapter 13). However, another case translated in this volume (pp. 135-147) is that of a young man, Chung Chih-min, who was sent to the countryside, gained preferential admission to the PLA, and subsequently entered Nanking University by the "back door," i.e., as a result of wirepulling by his powerful father. His application to withdraw was given nationwide publicity during the campaign to criticize Lin Piao and Confucius in early 1974. The two articles by Chung Chin-min depict vividly the poignant confrontation between the new official values, and the values of family continuity. A remarkable feature of this case is the generalizations in which it is couched, suggesting that the practice of going by the "back door" has in fact been a widespread one and that therefore a substantial gap between rhetoric and reality has existed with regard to this issue.

The ideological goals of the revolution in education and of the transfer program are linked to developmental goals. The re-

quirement that youths with secondary education integrate with
workers and peasants is an outgrowth of China's developmental
strategy, which places much stress on applied technology and
on diffusion of practical knowledge, particularly in the villages.
To this end, secondary education has been given a practical and
vocational orientation rather than a college-preparatory one.
Also, enrollment in secondary education has expanded greatly
while enrollment in higher schools is still below the levels
reached before the Cultural Revolution. The result is that
China has avoided a situation common to many third world
countries, in which a great many young people are educated in
middle and higher schools in subjects that are largely irrele-
vant to the needs of development, thereby leading to the widespread phenomenon of unemployment among the educated. At
the same time, China's approach to education has also led to
problems, particularly with regard to the quality of higher education. The greater vocational orientation of secondary schools
and the long hiatus between graduation from middle school and
admission to higher school has resulted in a drop in the quality
of the student body. Serious questions have been raised about
China's future supply of topflight scientists and engineers. (9)
Yet, attempts to tighten admissions standards have run into
objections from China's radicals who have charged that this
would endanger the egalitarian anti-elitist goals of the "revolution in education." The article reprinted on pp. 131-134 of
this volume reflects this conflict. It concerns a sent-down
youth in a Liaoning village, Chang T'ieh-sheng, who took entrance tests in physics and chemistry in 1973, when the State
Council had decreed a partial restoration of entrance examinations. Chang, who claimed that he had been unable to prepare
for the test because he was spending all his time on production
and political work, was unable to answer the questions. Instead, he polemicized against the examination, charging that
it played into the hands of bourgeois-type careerists scheming
to get into college. His case was publicized and despite his
academic weaknesses, he was admitted to a college. In November 1976, after Mao's death and the fall of four major leftist

leaders, Chang was accused of being a fraud whose ambitions
had been nurtured by supporters of the "gang of four" in Liaoning Province. (10) His case illustrates the problem of how to
reconcile the ideological quest for a nonelitist educational system with the need for high academic standards in at least some
components of that system.

When urban school graduates are sent to the countryside, it
is expected that they will make contributions to the development
of the locale in which they settle. These contributions can take
a variety of forms. Youth groups can reclaim a piece of land,
they can construct a small hydroelectric power station, groups
or individuals can take part in "scientific experiment," i.e.,
attempt to apply scientific knowledge to local conditions, or
they can contribute by teaching in locally run community
schools, by serving as barefoot doctors, or as agricultural
technicians. This volume, in fact, provides a good many examples of the kinds of contributions which sent-down youths
have been making to rural development and of the leaders that
have emerged from among them. The case of Hou Chün —
Chapter 7 — is an outstanding example of a young woman, who
in 1962 left Peking, settled in a brigade in Pao-ti hsien (now
part of Tientsin Municipality), took part in scientific experiment, ultimately emerging as a generalist, innovative leader.
The materials in this volume, however, also suggest that the
extent of the contributions has not been as great as in principle
possible. Why this has been the case requires examination of
the workings of the program in the countryside.

Operations of the Program

The history of the transfer movement since the Cultural
Revolution can been divided into two stages, with 1973 as the
dividing line. Until then, there had been the mass transfer in
the wake of the Cultural Revolution, but the rate had slowed
down in the early 1970s. Moreover, a good many problems
had arisen in the workings of the program. Sometime in 1973,
a decision was made to step up the transfer again. At the same

time, a decision was made to take much more substantial steps
than hitherto in making the program work. This remedial effort was apparently undertaken on the initiative of Mao Tse-
tung. In October 1972, a primary school teacher in a Fukien
town had sent Mao a letter complaining that his son who was
in a village was unable to make a living, requiring the father
to send regular remittances. The father was worried, because
what would become of his son after his death? In April 1973,
Mao reportedly sent the teacher a gift of 300 yuan, but more
importantly, he sent a letter in which he said that something
would be done. (11) And indeed, substantial remedial measures were taken that year. The book which forms the bulk
of this volume, Have a Warm Concern for the Growth of Educated Youths Going down to the Countryside, was published in
1973 and it reflects the remedial interests of the time. The
book contains one of the very few People's Daily editorials
published on the topic of sent-down youths. The editorial
vigorously reaffirmed the nation's commitment to the program.
It acknowledged the existence of problems, making clear that
vigorous efforts must be made to deal with them. The book
contains a number of major case studies reprinted from the
national or local press, in which problems are depicted and
model solutions outlined.

As the exchange of letters between the Fukien teacher and
Chairman Mao suggests, a major problem was that of self-
sufficiency of sent-down youths. In 1973 the press unambigu-
ously acknowledged the extent of the problem in an article reprinted as Chapter 3 of the book, in which it is noted that in
1970 "most" sent-down youths in one commune in Hopei had
been unable to make a living. Why? To begin with, the sent-
down youths worked about a third fewer days than did the peasants, hence earning fewer work points. One reason why they
might have been reluctant to work hard was that the local
cadres and peasants discriminated against them. Male urban
youths got two work points fewer than peasants for doing the
same work, and female sent-down youths one point fewer. And,
the urban youths were not benefiting from the sideline occupa-

tions that are a very important source of income for peasants.
Many failed to cultivate private vegetable plots or to raise
privately owned pigs.

The problems of self-sufficiency was linked to inadequate
leadership. A theme that runs through several of the articles
reproduced in the book is that local leaders, from the county
down to the production team, often regarded the sent-down
youths as a burden rather than a blessing. The management
of their affairs required time and effort and interfered with
the performance of the "central tasks" which necessarily must
take priority. Consequently, the rural leadership core, the
Party committees and Party secretaries, tended not to deal
with settlement issues, preferring to delegate these matters
to minor functionaries. The indifference of higher-level cadres
made discriminatory practices possible and also contributed
to a failure to devise arrangements that would permit sent-
down youths to benefit from subsidiary income sources.

Another problem was that of adequacy of the resources com-
mitted to the program. Settling the young migrants obviously
costs money. The state provides a settlement fee for each urban youth sent to the countryside with which to pay for housing,
small tools, and rations during an initial adjustment period
when it is not expected that sent-down youths will be able to
work as hard as the peasants. Prior to 1973, this was reportedly 230 yuan per youth. (12) Often, however, it was not sufficient to cover the cost of building simple houses for youth
groups, giving rise to the issue of who is to make up the short-
age. Several of the articles in the book describe the problem.
In I-ch'eng hsien, Shansi, "Some of the cadres felt that we
should build no more houses for the educated than those for
which the higher levels had allocated money." As a model
case the question was naturally resolved in favor of doing a
proper job. "In 1969, in addition to the amount allotted by the
country for building housing, we ourselves made more than
700,000 chin of lime, baked more than 100,000 bricks and quarried more than 100 pieces of stone. In 1,500 work hours, we
built for the educated youths ten caves lined with bricks and

five tiled houses" (p. 98). Similarly, in Feng-jun hsien, Hopei,
some brigades decided, after much debate, to "raise some
money for building houses" in 1965, when a batch of urban
youths was assigned to them. In 1970, more of them came and
again the question of housing arose. "This time, it is not necessary to build houses again. Let's give the money to the production team to develop production," i.e., divert the settlement
fee to productive uses of general benefit (pp. 66-67). The Party
branch successfully opposed this proposal but the fact that it
was made gives an indication that in some cases the state settlement fee was misappropriated and diverted to other uses.
But apparently, the prevailing pattern has been that the receiving rural units have had to chip in their own resources, if only
in the form of labor. Undoubtedly, this has been a source of
resentment in at least some cases.

Still another problem was that in a number of villages, sent-
down youths were not utilized to maximum effectiveness. In
part this was due to their own inadequacies. It seems that their
schooling had not always prepared them to play a meaningful
role in the countryside. Often they lacked not only concrete
applied skills but even basic book knowledge. Probably the
latter was most often so in the case of the Red Guard generation, whose middle school education had been abbreviated by
the outbreak of the Cultural Revolution, even though they were
in 1968 declared middle school graduates. The most striking
example of their shortcomings in this regard appears on
pp. 61-62, where a group of youths is described who tried to
graft cotton shoots onto a paulownia tree in order to produce
a "cotton tree" that would yield annual harvests of cotton without replanting. The projects which these young urbanites under-
took evidently wasted brigade resources and largely led to nothing, until the local leaders provided better guidance. In any
event, a good many locals seem to have gotten the impression
that the sent-down youths were neither able nor willing to contribute much to rural progress: "... some people only saw
faults in the educated youths ... and did not see their good points;
they always emphasized that they had little experience in struggle,

that they were clumsy in their work, and that they were unwilling to let go and really work" (p. 13).

As the preceding quote suggests, local responses to the urban youths as troublesome burdens were in part based on the perceptions that the youths were often poorly motivated. The sources of poor morale lay in the hardships of rural life, such as the lower standard of living, the greater monotony, the hard work, and also, at least in some cases, in the frustration engendered by discrimination against even those youths who did try to do well. A major aspect of poor morale was a sense of relative deprivation: "Some classmates have entered the factories in the cities, while all day long we deal with this wretched land, what's the point!" (p. 64). To some degree, good morale and good performance could be elicited by holding out the possibility of reassignment to the urban sector, for the indefinite, for-life commitment demanded of the sent-down youths was the most basic source of poor morale. Disappointment at not being selected, however, could exacerbate poor morale: "Last year, when the brigade selected two educated youths to go to factories to become workers, the event caused some...to vacillate in their thinking. They felt that a 'worker has a future; being left behind in the villages is so unpromising'" (pp. 96-97). Sometimes a sent-down youth did extremely well in the countryside, becoming a cadre or making an important contribution, but the underlying calculation was that doing well would earn him a return ticket to the city. In one such case reported in this book the individual was denied reassignment because she had acquired value to the local community, leading her to complain that "advancement is a drawback" (p. 15).

In the second half of 1973, the nation's leaders took steps to improve the workings of the program. National, provincial, and local conferences dealt with issues of the settlement, thereby greatly raising the visibility and salience of the problems of sent-down youths. Party committees and secretaries were told to devote regular attention to them and to take steps to improve the management of their affairs. They were told to conduct inspections in order to uncover and to end discriminatory

treatment and other abuses. With regard to the latter, it is
noteworthy that the People's Daily editorial spoke of the necessity "fiercely to attack those class enemies and criminal elements that persecute and destroy educated youths" (p. 6).

Undoubtedly, in 1973, the rural leadership hierarchy was to
a significant extent mobilized to deal with the settlement, but
there is also reason to believe that it has been difficult to sustain an adequate level of attention, simply because other tasks
necessarily must take priority. Thus, in one of the cases reported here, once a set of problems had been resolved, "some
of the leading comrades in the commune again began to relax,
feeling that having special persons responsible for grasping
this task was sufficient" (p. 33). Similarly, a Red Flag article
published in 1975 complained that "some comrades are merely
content with 'welcoming' the educated youths," noting that some
cadres continued to view the task of dealing with them as an additional burden (pp. 162-3). Perhaps because there are inher-
ent difficulties in securing ongoing rural leadership involvement with the affairs of sent-down youths, the practice was
publicized in 1974 and 1975 of sending urban cadres on long-
term assignments to the rural areas to help with the settlement
of the youths. In 1975 alone, 60,000 urban cadres were assigned
to this task (p. 169).

Improved, ongoing leadership and guidance were related to
increasing the capacity of the sent-down youths to be self-
sufficient and earn a living on par with that of the peasants.
One of the reasons why sent-down youths had worked fewer
days than peasants was simply that supervision was lax. Those
able to live off their families could choose whether or not to go
out to work. Tightened control, e.g., the introduction of "work
checks" (p. 55), resulted in more days worked. Further, an effort was made to collectivize the lives of the urban youths. In
the past many, though living in small groups in production
teams, had tried to subsist as individuals. This meant that they
frequently lacked the time or the inclination to cultivate a vegetable plot or raise privately owned pigs, which a peasant household's division of labor makes possible. Wide promotion of

"collective households," "youth points," and "youth farms"
was designed to make it possible for the youths to carry on
sideline productive activities on a collective basis, thereby en-
suring that they would benefit from this crucial source of income. In general, there has been a tendency to concentrate
youth settlements by establishing, to the extent possible, separate youth farms attached to but separate from peasant production teams or brigades. The article "A Very Good Model"
(pp. 148 ff.) describes how this was done in one location, Chu-
chou, Hunan. The goal is not only to utilize the young people
for purposes of land reclamation, but to subject them to more
carefully structured organizational influences.

The remedial campaign also entailed allocation of additional
resources to the transfer program. Reportedly, the settlement
fee was just about doubled. The county authorities were assigned a much greater share of the responsibility for housing
construction in order to reduce the burdens on the communes,
especially their lower divisions. In addition, ad hoc arrangements have been made to mobilize resources from the urban
sector in order to meet the needs of the youth settlements. In
Chu-chou, Hunan, for example, "when the building materials
were insufficient, the factory... used its own materials; when
problems of transportation came up, the... factory would send
trucks out to help" (p. 155). To a significant extent, the additional resources have permitted construction of adequate housing. In Chi hsien, Hopei, for instance, a substantial effort was
made to build houses for long-term settlement of sent-down
youths. Provision was also made for housing married urban
youths (see Chapter 3). Apparently, similar efforts were made
elsewhere as well.

Chinese policy-makers also sought to tap the talents of the
sent-down youths more effectively than had hitherto been the
case. As the editorial pointed out, "For agriculture to improve... it is necessary for large number of educated youths
to take the political, cultural, and scientific knowledge that they
have acquired and unite it with the realities of the village class
struggle and socialist agricultural production and contribute

their strength to build new socialist villages" (p. 4). Some
local cadres learned that "to see only the faults of the educated
youths . . . and not be willing to use them is completely wrong"
(p. 14). "Bold use" has three components. First, some outstanding young people who have proved themselves are selected
to cadre positions and to membership in the CCP, some of them
becoming innovative generalist leaders of their villages. The
number of such cases is quite small on a national scale but can
be quite significant locally. One index is Party membership.
As of the end of 1974, 70,000 of the 10 million sent-down youths
had joined the CCP (.7 percent) (p. 170). In Huai-te hsien, Kirin, however, 28 sent-down youths out of 345 joined the CCP,
or 8.1 percent (p. 29). In Hai-ch'eng hsien, Liaoning, where
an unusually large number of youths had settled, over 50,000
as of 1976, 1,200 had joined the CCP (pp. 188-192). In Hai-
ch'eng, moreover, it was reported in 1975 that one tenth of that
county's production teams, 300 in all, were headed by sent-
down youths (p. 186). This too is a remarkable result and has
not been replicated elsewhere. Perhaps it has something to do
with the earthquake that struck Hai-ch'eng in early 1975. The
point is that there are cases of young urbanites who attain significant rural leadership positions by dint of their capacities
and their dedication, even though the proportion of all sent-
down youths playing leadership roles is not great. In addition,
however, a good many cases have been publicized in which
youth groups play collective leadership roles, for example in
transforming a backward team or even a brigade into an advanced one.

Second, "bold use" entails mobilizing youths to contribute
their technical or scientific knowledge to the local community.
As noted previously, what the urban youths know is not always
adequate to the purposes of local innovation or to adaptation of
scientific knowledge to local conditions. In order to correct
these deficiencies, numerous short-term study programs have
been instituted in recent years within the communes and at the
county level, both for sent-down youths and for local people.
As the country's commitment to achieving the modernization

of agriculture gains momentum at the local level, it is likely
that such learning opportunities will proliferate, thereby enabling the educated youths to participate more effectively in
the scientific and technical transformation of their villages.
And third, there is collective labor, which, as a good many of
the selections in this volume show, is a major component of
the activities of the urban youth. Collective labor projects are
central to China's rural development effort, since they emphasize such tasks as leveling of land or terracing of hillsides,
using human labor as a key input. (13)

In the official point of view, the single most important remedial measure has always been political education of the
sent-down youths. Political education was stressed not only
in 1973; it has been a central theme during the entire transfer
movement. Certainly in the materials here reproduced, political education is given enormous prominence. The purpose of
political education is not only to change the world outlook of
the young urbanites, but specifically to combat the morale
crises that periodically recur among many of them. Thus when
some youths in Feng-jun hsien began to waver in their commitment, having already labored in the village for six or seven
years, the remedy of choice was to teach the youths about the
ideals of communism, thereby strengthening their determination to stay (pp. 64-65). Often a political lesson consists of
education in the history of local class struggle, accompanied
by i-k'u ssu-t'ien, recalling of past bitterness and comparing
it with present sweetness, in which peasants will tell of the
hardships and exploitation to which they were subjected before
liberation. One of the themes in political education is that it
is easy for local class enemies to demoralize the young urbanites. In one such case, a counterrevolutionary caused "confusion" among some youths by telling them: "Your family is
really so bitter! If you were in town, living with your father
and mother, eating good rice and good dishes, then you would
not be as you are now" (p. 58). Because political education
must address itself to the continuing attraction of urban life,
it is directed not only at the youths in the countryside but at

their families in the cities as well. Chapter 8 deals with the
role of the cadres of neighborhood organizations in a Shanghai
district, who educate the parents of sent-down youths to take
a proper attitude toward their offspring, reinforcing their determination to take root in the countryside.

As Chinese policy-makers themselves have recognized, even
the most intensive political education cannot suffice to sustain
the morale of the sent-down youths. Ongoing efforts are required to make their living conditions tolerable, to provide
mobility opportunities within the rural sector and outlets for
their creative energies, as well as a satisfactory cultural and
recreational life. To these requirements can be added the opportunity to get married. As the sent-down youths mature and
reach the official marriage age, the extent to which conditions
are created that facilitate marriage obviously becomes an important issue. During and since the remedial campaign, some
attention was paid to this matter, as the chapter on Chi hsien
shows (Chapter 3), and the important article in the Appendix,
"Have a Warm Concern for the Growth of Married Educated
Youths Who Have Gone Down to the Countryside" (pp. 173-83).
These materials indicate that the proportion of marriages is
not very high and that new problems, such as those of housing,
childcare, and political participation arise.

It is not easy to answer the question of whether the transfer
movement is a success in the sense that the problems that have
arisen have been successfully solved and that more and more
sent-down youths are adapting to rural life. The evidence is
often too fragmentary to permit generalization. On balance, it
would seem fair to say that significant improvements have
taken place, but a good deal of evidence also suggests that
problems in the settlement of the young urbanites have persisted. Their most important source is the continuing gap between popular preferences and the official values. As a broadcast made in 1975 put it:

Why is it that some comrades regard the settlement of
educated young people ... merely as a stopgap measure....

Why is it that some parents invariably want to keep their children in town and do not let them take root in the countryside? Why is it that some educated young people only want to steel themselves for a few years in the country-side...but do not want to...work there for their entire lives? All this is because they have not mastered the theory of the dictatorship of the proletariat.... They do not realize that settlement of educated young people in the countryside is a hundred-year stratagem for narrowing the three big gaps and restricting bourgeois rights. (14)

If it is true to say that this gap will persist until rural-urban conditions have in fact been equalized, then it can be suggested that even if remedial measures continue to be taken, the implementation of the program will continue to be plagued by difficulties.

Notes

1) For discussion of all aspects of the program, see Thomas P. Bernstein, Up to the Mountains and Down to the Villages: The Transfer of Youth from Urban to Rural China (New Haven: Yale University Press, 1977).

2) The New York Times, December 13, 1976, p. 3.

3) For discussion of this value conflict, see Chapter III of Bernstein, Up to the Mountains.

4) Shih Ling, "Chien-ch'ih ch'ing-nien t'ung kung-nung chieh-ho ti cheng-ch'üeh lu-hsien," (Persist in the correct line of youth integrating with the workers and peasants), Hung-ch'i, No. 12 (December 1, 1975), p. 30.

5) Frederick C. Teiwes, "The Assignment of University Graduates in China, 1974," The China Quarterly, No. 62 (June 1975), pp. 308-9.

6) For more discussion, see Chapter VI of Bernstein, Up to the Mountains.

7) Ibid., Chapter II.

8) Chih-nung hung-ch'i, No. 3 (November 1, 1967), in

Translations on Communist China: Political and Sociological, No. 436 (January 17, 1968), JPRS, No. 44052.

9) See Robert Scalapino, "The Struggle over Higher Education: Revolution vs. Development," Issues & Studies, Vol. 12, No. 7 (July 1976), pp. 1-8.

10) For one denunciation of Chang T'ieh-sheng, see Jenmin jih-pao, November 30, 1976.

11) This is reported by Chinese emigres interviewed in Hong Kong. The PRC press has described the exchange of letters, but has not made the content public. See for instance, Radio Foochow, April 25, 1974, in Foreign Broadcast Information Service (FBIS) No. 92 (May 10, 1974), and Radio Foochow, May 4, 1974, in FBIS No. 88 (May 6, 1974).

12) The amount is reported by informants interviewed in Hong Kong. The press refers to the settlement fee, but only indirectly.

13) For extended discussion of the developmental impact of the sent-down youths, see Bernstein, Up to the Mountains, Chapter V.

14) Radio Changsha, May 14, 1975, in FBIS, No. 95 (May 15, 1975).

The Rustication
of Urban Youth
in China

1

Make Progress in Doing a Good Job with Educated
Youths Who Have Gone up to the Mountains and
down to the Countryside

A <u>People's Daily</u> Editorial*

The movement of educated youths up to the mountains and down
to the countryside is a great event in our country's socialist revolution and socialist construction. Under the great call of Chairman
Mao for "educated youths to go to the villages," several million
young students, their hearts full of revolutionary fervor, have gone
in the last few years to the rural villages and border areas, to
the people's communes and production and construction brigades,
and to state farms to unite with the workers and peasants.
Under the leadership of the Party, they have experienced
the winds and rains of the Three Great Revolutionary Movements
and have seen the world; large numbers of progressive collectives, as well as progressive individuals like Hsing Yen-tzu and

---

*Jen-min jih-pao she-lun. "Chin-i-pu tso-hao chih-shih
ch'ing-nien shang-shan hsia-hsiang ti kung-tso."

3

Hou Chün, have emerged. Some have joined the Chinese Communist Party and Communist Youth League; some have joined the ranks of leadership at all levels; some have undertaken work of all kinds at the basic level; and many have come up with inventive creations. They have become an enthusiastic and lively force for socialist revolution and socialist construction in the villages. Facts have fully proved that "the villages are a vast universe where one can be of great use." The roiling revolutionary flood of educated youths going up to the mountains and down to the countryside has fiercely attacked the thought and habits of several thousands years of contempt for peasants and labor by the exploiting class, and has been very useful in changing customs and traditions and reforming society. It has made the relationship between town and country more intimate, has strengthened the alliance between workers and peasants, and has already had, and will continue to have, a deep effect on the politics, ideology, economics, and culture of our nation.

Every year in our country there are so many young students who go up to the mountains and down to the countryside and vividly experience the outstanding nature of our socialist system. Agriculture is the foundation of the people's economy. The condition of agriculture is closely related to the development of our country's socialist revolution and socialist construction. For agriculture to improve, for the villages to change their appearance, it is necessary for large numbers of educated youths to take the political, cultural, and scientific knowledge that they have acquired and unite it with the realities of village class struggle and socialist agricultural production and contribute their strength to build new socialist villages. Many poor and lower-middle peasants have put it well: "The villages need educated youths." The educated youths who go to the countryside have, from their earliest youth, grown up in the cities and seldom come into contact with village society. To send them when they are grown to the villages to be tempered and grow is an important path for cultivating and creating successors to the proletarian revolutionary cause. The villages are also universities. There, the young people find infinite knowledge and infinite work to be done. After the educated youths have been reeducated by the poor and lower-middle peasants, they gradually become one with the working people; and when they have been tempered by the Three Great Revolutionary Movements of class struggle, production struggle, and scientific experiment, they can become workers who have socialist consciousness and who are cultured. Many educated youths have also put it well: "We need the villages even more." The two "needs" of the poor and lower-middle peasants and the educated youths are imperative for continuing the revolution under the proletarian dictatorship, for strengthening the economic foundation and the superstructure of socialism, and for strengthening the dictatorship of the proletariat and preventing the revival of capitalism. In the last analysis they mean to implement Chairman Mao's words, "Practice Marxism; don't practice revisionism."

Since the movement of educated youths up to the mountains and down to the countryside is a great socialist revolution, it cannot but struggle with the two types of thought, two classes, and two lines. Leaders at every level must use the Party's basic line for the entire socialist historical stage to understand and deal with this revolution. Comrades who firmly carry out the revolutionary line of Chairman Mao have to totally support this revolution. They should consider doing a good job in up to the mountains and down to the countryside work to be an important cause to grasp for consolidating and developing the great results of the Proletarian Cultural Revolution. Our masses of cadres are doing precisely this; many comrades even enthusiastically send their sons and daughters to engage in agriculture, becoming models setting an example. It is worth mentioning that there are a few comrades who still do not comprehend this revolution and who are not achieving their potential. We hope that they will quickly change. To work with educated youths who go up to the mountains and down to the countryside, one must stand for principle and firmly resist wrong. In the management and education of educated youths who are going to the countryside and returning to the countryside, we must exercise the political leadership of the proletariat and must do very careful ideological and political work. Young people are the most willing to learn and have the least conservative thinking; their main direction is good. We must resolutely protect and support the revolutionary spirit of educated youths and listen to their opinions and requests. We must seriously study particular methods to develop the strength of young people, actively cultivate them, and not look upon them as one and destroy their individuality.

To do a good job of working with educated youths going up to the mountains and down to the countryside, we must use the principle of rectification through criticism of revisionism. We must criticize the reactionary and fallacious statements of swindlers like Liu Shao-ch'i who have trumpeted "study to become an official," "go to the countryside to acquire gold-plating," and "it is disguised reform through labor." We must expose the true rightest nature of their counterrevolutionary revisionist line, and clean out its flowing poison. We must be vigilant against the disrupting activities of class enemies. We must fiercely attack those class enemies and criminal elements that persecute and destroy educated youths and must use the law to punish them in order to truly assure the healthy growth of the younger generation.

Cadres on every level must earnestly practice Chairman Mao's directives; they must have a unified plan to solve the problems encountered in the advancement of educated youths going to the countryside; they must carry out every Party policy in order to help educated youths put down roots in the villages. We must organize educated youths to read conscientiously books by Marx and Lenin and books by Chairman Mao, to study cultural, scientific and technical knowledge and vigorously cultivate their proletarian world view so that they will take the "red and expert" road. Educated youths who have gone to the countryside must also be concerned with the socialist revolution in the superstructure and with the class struggle between the proletariat and the bourgeoisie in the ideological realm. They must learn to distinguish between materialism and idealism, between

Marxism and revisionism. They must resolutely struggle against incorrect thoughts and incorrect tendencies that obstruct the progress of socialism and do not contribute to the consolidation of the dictatorship of the proletariat. We must enthusiastically and seriously develop those educated youths who meet the requirements for Party and League membership. We must pay attention to cultivating cadres from among the educated youths. For sons and daughters who can be properly educated, we must emphasize political behavior. We must teach the young people to struggle bitterly, to join in labor enthusiastically, and to make a great effort to expand production. We must patiently direct the production of the young people, concern ourselves with their lives, and pay attention to combining labor and leisure. We must look after the special physiology of young women when delegating farming activities. When these matters are carried out, we can more ably encourage young people to take the path of unity with workers and peasants.

A summary of our experience in the past several years indicates that the key to doing a good job in the movement of educated youth up to the mountains and down to the countryside is Party leadership. Party committees on every level must strengthen their leadership, make strict examinations, sum up experiences, draw up plans, and assiduously do good work. The Communist Youth League and Women's Association must make it their responsibility to spread education about solidarity to the educated youths going to the countryside and returning to the countryside. To mobilize people in the town and in the area receiving the youth so that they complement each other closely, it is necessary to send some cadres whose thoughts and actions are good, and who are capable, to lead the educated youths. Revolutionary parents must help comrades in the villages by giving ideological education to their sons and daughters. Comrades in villages everywhere must improve management and educational work with educated youths who have gone to, or have returned to, the countryside. The cultural publishing system ought to produce more reading materials for educated youths. Each line of battle, each office, must concertedly com-

plement each other in order to cultivate the contributory
strength of the successors to the revolution. The educated
youths are the precious treasure of the Party and the country;
let us feel a sense of political obligation for the work of the
Party, and a high spirit of responsibility for the next generation
of proletarians; let us have a warm regard for their growth, and
make progress in up to the mountains down to the countryside
work.

Young comrades going to the countryside and returning to
the countryside: Chairman Mao, the Party Central Committee,
and the people of the entire country are all concerned about
you and have entrusted in you their great hopes. Beginning
from today, the period of fifty to a hundred years will be a great
period of earthshaking changes. The appearance of our nation,
and especially the appearance of the villages, will undergo extremely great changes. The young people must put down roots
and grow in the villages with brave hearts and strong wills.
Together with the masses of poor and lower-middle peasants,
they must initiate a powerful movement to learn from Tachai
in agriculture, be self-reliant, and struggle bitterly in order
to make an even greater contribution in carrying out the revolutionary line of Chairman Mao, achieving the modernization
of agriculture, and completing the historical mission of constructing a new socialist countryside.

August 7, 1973

2

The Great Task of Cultivating Successors
to the Proletarian Revolutionary Cause

Chinese Communist Party
Ming-shui <u>Hsien</u> Committee*

Since 1968 Ming-shui <u>hsien</u>, Heilungkiang Province, has had
more than a thousand educated youths go to the countryside to
join the brigades and make a home. In the past several years,
our <u>hsien</u> committee has followed our great leader Chairman
Mao's instruction that "we must concern ourselves with the
growth of the young generation," and has regarded the work of
continuing to educate educated youths who have gone to the countryside as an important task for cultivating successors to the proletarian revolutionary cause; thus we have unceasingly strengthened the leadership of the Party, leading the young people to
earnestly read books and study, and enthusiastically join in the

---

*Chung-kuo kung-ch'an-tang Ming-shui hsien wei-yüan-hui,
"P'ei-yang wu-ch'an-chieh-chi ko-ming shih-yeh chieh-pan-jen
ti i-chien ta-shih."

9

Three Great Revolutionary Movements, so that they may become useful in the struggle to build new socialist villages.

Chairman Mao says, "The line is a principle; the principle establishes the objective." Thinking back on the work of these years, we are able more deeply to understand that only by fiercely adhering to the line and correctly treating educated youths who go to the countryside can we thoroughly strengthen the leadership of the Party and do a good job of educating educated youths who have gone up to the mountains and down to the countryside.

A High Level of Seriousness Will Be Achieved Only through Correct Treatment

In December 1968 Chairman Mao directed: "Educated youths must go to the villages and receive reeducation from the poor and lower-middle peasants. . . . Comrades from villages everywhere should welcome their going." The great masses of educated youths enthusiastically responded to Chairman Mao's great call and in great numbers went to the countryside to join the brigades and make a home. At the time, because the hsien committee's understanding of Chairman Mao's directive was not deep, we did not fully understand the great significance of sending educated youths up to the mountains and down to the countryside. We felt that our central work task was already heavy, that there were many ways to form a battle line, and that working with educated youth was a local matter and handing it over to the vocational bureau should take care of it. For all these reasons, we naively regarded the important matter of sending educated youths up to the mountains and down to the countryside as a question of the disposition of labor forces and seldom inquired about it. Not long afterward the reality of class struggle and line struggle aroused our deep thoughts and all matters concerning the advancement of young people greatly inspired us.

Let us take as an example the No. 8 Production Team of Tung-fang-hung Brigade, Sheng-li Commune. In the spring of

1969, because of the disruption of a small group of class enemies, the leading elements were paralyzed, and there was no
one to harvest the spring crop. An educated youth, Wang Ke-
min, who joined the brigade here bravely took up the heavy burden of leadership of the production team. He confidently accepted the leadership of the brigade Party branch, strongly relied on the poor and lower-middle peasants, and began a
struggle against class enemies. After a year of hard work, of
grasping the revolution and promoting production, the appearance of the No. 8 Team underwent a profound change. In the midst
of struggle it formed a strong leadership, and the production of
food increased 40 percent over the previous year.

Reality caused us gradually to understand that among the
masses of educated youths who have gone to the countryside
there is stored an enormous amount of socialist activism. Certainly we cannot simply use them as a labor source; we should
also cultivate them as the successors to the proletarian revolution. Whether one takes seriously working with educated
youths who have gone to the countryside is an important question
of whether one has a high line consciousness, and whether one
has political farsightedness. The comrades of the hsien committee say with deep feeling. "The matter of educated youths
going to the countryside is relevant to the general situation, to
the future of the proletarian revolution. We must use the power
of one generation to plan for the welfare of several generations.
Starting with the goal of consolidating the dictatorship of the
proletariat with constructing socialism, we must earnestly do
a good job of working with educated youths who have gone to
the countryside." With this type of understanding, our hsien
committee adopted a series of measures to strengthen thoroughly the leadership for work with educated youths.

First, we placed this task on the hsien committee's agenda of
important matters and appointed a member of the standing committee to take specific responsibility for holding collective discussion of important matters and quickly resolving problems.

Second, each commune and each brigade set up "three-in-one"
leadership units, and each youth point [ch'ing nien tien] selected

two cadres who had joined the brigades to take leadership responsibility. Thus, someone grasped this work at every level, and all matters were transmitted down to each location. In addition, the hsien committee scheduled periodic investigations of organizations, frequently held on-site conferences, organized learning through observation, and exchanged experience in working with educated youths.

Third, when the hsien committee leads comrades and cadres from agencies to the countryside, they all go to the youth points to observe and to help the young people solve questions of thought, production, and livelihood. The secretary of the hsien committee each year continues to go to the youth point to celebrate with the educated youths the Spring Festival in revolutionary style, to remember with the young people past bitterness and think of the present sweetness, to sit and talk, and to learn from the harvest of the past year.

Fourth, our hsien committee leads cadres to regard their leadership in being the first to send their sons and daughters to the countryside as a matter of important principle in implementing Chairman Mao's revolutionary line, as a single revolution for washing away old thoughts, and as a deep criticism of swindlers like Liu Shao-ch'i. Thus in mobilizing educated youths to go up to the mountains and down to the countryside, they can set an example by taking the lead in sending sons and daughters to engage in agriculture. In the past few years, of the sons and daughters of the members of the standing committee of the hsien, those who should go to the countryside have all gone to the villages. In this way, they not only set an example for the cadres of various agencies and the parents of the masses of educated youths, they also advanced revolution in the thinking of the hsien committee.

Bold Implementation Will Be Achieved
Only through Correct Treatment

"Of all social forces, youths are the most active and most vital force. They are the most willing to learn, and they have

the least conservative thinking; this is especially true in the
socialist period." We gradually deepened our understanding of
this directive of Chairman Mao while carrying it out.

Because some of the brigades in our hsien were influenced by
erroneous tendencies in society, some people only saw faults
in the educated youths who came to the countryside and did not
see their good points; they always emphasized that they had
little experience in struggle, that they were clumsy in their
work, and that they were unwilling to let go and really work.
This suppressed the revolutionary fervor of many youths.

In contrast, some brigades emphasized developing the usefulness of the educated youths and gained very good results.
For example, Ching-feng Brigade in the spring of 1968 had
thirty-eight educated youths who came to join the brigade; the
Party branch of the brigade selected eight old poor peasants
to lead them to a wild stretch of land five or six li from the village to set up a K'angta Youth Brigade.* Through self-reliance
and hard struggle, they opened up more than 1,500 mou** of land
in the wilderness. That year they were able to give to the country 80,000 chin of food crops, and in subsequent years, were
able to give close to 100,000 chin a year. In the hardship of establishing something, the young people underwent much tempering, and thus became a group of progressive elements. Some
participated in the viewing ceremony of the celebrations of the
twentieth year of the establishment of the People's Republic of
China; some joined leadership groups of various levels; many
took responsibility for technical work. They became a progressive body of educated youths in the countryside for the entire province. The Party branch of Kuang-hua Brigade persistently organized educated youths in the countryside to run
a "May 7" evening school, and promoted for the entire brigade
a mass movement to study Marxism-Leninism-Mao Tsetung
Thought, thus advancing unceasing progress in revolution and
production. The Party branch of Shih-fan Brigade organized

*See the Glossary.
**See the Glossary.

the educated youths in the countryside to carry out scientific experiments on a large scale with the poor and lower-middle peasants, causing the entire brigade to plant crops scientifically and increasing the production of food crops manyfold.

Two ways of doing things, two different results: in the process, we have learned that to see only the faults of educated youths in the countryside and not be willing to use them is completely wrong. Only through bold use can the educated youths experience tempering in the great winds and waves of revolution, grow in ability, and perform great deeds; and only through bold use can we help educated youths in the process of reconstructing the objective world, accepting reeducation, and reconstructing their worldviews. From now on we will consider the maximum use of educated youths an important ring to grasp in the work of administering education. In the past few years the hsien has recommended and helped 193 educated youths to join the leadership units of the region, the hsien, the commune, the brigade, and the production team; more than 310 educated youths have become tutors in the study of Chairman Mao's works, bookkeepers for production brigades, security persons, cashiers, agricultrual technicians, tractor operators, barefoot doctors, teachers at popularly managed schools, etc.; among them many are rated as activists and labor models. Some of the young people are exuberant in spirit, unafraid to think and to do, and in agricultural production and every aspect of work they have made notable contributions.

Persistence in Education Will Be Achieved Only through Correct Treatment

The basic nature and main tendencies of the masses of educated youths in the countryside are good, but there are also some weak points and faults. To emphasize bold use does not mean that we can let go and not concern ourselves anymore. Carrying out the reeducation of educated youths and fully developing their usefulness are mutually dependent and mutually restrictive. The educated youths come to the villages to receive reeducation and to fully develop their usefulness. The goal of

education is to allow them to develop better their usefulness in
the Three Great Revolutionary Movements and fully become
successors to the proletarian revolutionary cause. Only by
persisting in education while they are being used can young
people be able to grow more quickly in the correct direction.

The hsien committee, besides educating cadres at every level, relying on the poor and lower-middle peasants, and persisting in reeducating educated youths in thought, labor, and livelihood, has especially emphasized organizing educated youths
in the countryside to join the acute and complicated class struggles in the villages, so that they may be tempered and grow in
struggle through wind and rain and seeing the world. Since
1969, our hsien has organized many educated youths to join the
"one strike, three anti" movement.* In response to the young people's lack of experience in struggle, the hsien committee
adopted the method of having the old lead the new, and selected
a few old cadres who have had struggle experiences to resolve
the problems appearing in the movement, to carry out with the
young people education in the Party's line and policies, helping
them strengthen their concept of class struggle and line struggle
and raising their political level.

Our hsien committee also emphatically advocated the con-
tinual development of progressive youths, fully allowing them
to become further advanced. The educated youth I Hsiu-lan,
after going to the countryside, progressed rather quickly, soon
joined the Youth League, and became head of the production
team. Then she saw that among the schoolmates who went to
the countryside with her, some had entered the university and
some had become industrial workers. She began to think that
"advancement is a drawback," and her energy for work was not
boundless as before. The Party secretary of the commune who
was working in the local area, Yu Yung-se, sought out little I
for heart-to-heart talks many times after he understood this
situation to help her correctly see the role of agricultural labor

---

*See the Glossary.

in socialism. She gradually embraced the ideology of walking the road of unity with workers and peasants forever. Since then, I Hsiu-lan has made strict demands on herself and has led the masses in grasping revolution and promoting production with abundant strength. Recently, she appeared with honor at the Heilungkiang Provincial Representative Assembly for Advanced Groups and Labor Models for Building Socialism.

As for the few backward educated youths, we do not neglect them; we do not look down on them, but follow Chairman Mao's directive to "be close to them, unite with them, persuade them, encourage them to advance." As a result, the more backward youths of the hsien have shown comparatively great progress. The educated youth point of Tsung-te Brigade had a "backward sharper" famous throughout the hsien. Some people suggested not worrying about him anymore, letting him go and forgetting about him. The secretary of the Party branch of the brigade, Tseng Yuan-cheng, was against it. He said, "If we don't concern ourselves about him, we are giving up our responsibility, we are giving up the struggle of fighting for the younger generation against the bourgeois classes." Tseng Yuan-ching used the point of view that "one divides into two" and carried out a complete analysis of this regressive youth: He was born into a worker's family which had suffered much bitterness, and his basic character is good; his bad thoughts are not innate but are the result of the aggression of bourgeois thought in society; we need only to patiently educate him and we can certainly change him. Starting with this knowledge, Tseng Yuan-ching, after half a year of difficult and detailed political thought work, finally helped this young person to change for the good. Later he even joined the Communist Youth League.

Enthusiastic Concern Will Be Achieved
Only through Correct Treatment

Just when young people are growing physically and intellectually, enthusiastic concern for their growth and active development of activities suited to their special qualities are aspects of good management of educational work that cannot be neglected and are also a necessary condition for promoting their long-term settlement in the villages to carry out revolution.

We must first show enthusiastic concern for the politics and thought of educated youth in the countryside. Important meetings of Party delegates, League delegates, and cadres that our hsien held all had Party members, League members, and cadre representatives from among the educated youths participating. We have actively, seriously, and at an appropriate time promoted Party and League membership for educated youths who meet the conditions for joining. In the past few years, the hsien absorbed 21 educated youths into the Chinese Communist Party and 389 into the Communist Youth League and was attentive to absorbing young women into the Party and the League. Educated youths are asked to deal with all sorts of activities. In order to satisfy the young people's desire for learning, to make them "both red and expert," we take responsibility for their study of books. At every youth point, we set up a library, order newspapers, and put in a broadcast speaker. We have a provision that every month there will be four or five afternoons devoted to studying politics, culture, and agricultural technology, and developing criticism of revisionism. Some youths also invite school teachers to lecture and to tutor them.

In the last two years, the hsien committee, concerned for the livelihood of educated youths in the countryside, has comprehensively distributed the youth points, in accordance with changing conditions, and has tried to send them to brigades where the leadership is strong and the potential for developing production is relatively great. The Party branch of Yuan-ta Brigade frequently encourages the young people to be self-sufficient and to raise their own standards of living. It mobilized them to find their own firewood, clean their houses, plant vegetables, and raise pigs, so that in the past few years they have accumulated altogether more than 1,400 yuan in living expenses and more than 1,200 chin of grain. After we had spread the experience of this brigade over the entire hsien, every youth point, with the help of the commune, the brigades, and the poor and lower-middle peasants, constructed spacious, light, sturdy, and warm living quarters, accumulated living expenses, had a surplus of grain, and were self-sufficient in meat and vegetables. More important, the educated youths have developed the good habits of bitter struggle, diligence, and frugality.

Because of the educated youths' energy, enjoyment of exercise, love of singing and other special qualities, we organized them to actively participate in cultural and physical activities. Every youth point acquired, as needed, some musical instruments and set up an amateur arts propaganda team. They wrote and acted in their own programs, using proletarian thought to conquer the literature and arts battlefield of the villages. Each youth point, using the simplest means, also built basketball courts, ping pong rooms, and other such physical sport facilities.

In order to ensure the healthy growth of educated youths in the countryside, the hsien committee has asked the concerned production teams to look after them appropriately when assigning work, going from simple to complex, and to make sure that work and leisure are united. When the educated youths are ill, they must be quickly treated. Because of the special physiology of female educated youths, it is provided that on certain days they will not do heavy work and will not be in water. With the warm concern of every level of Party organization and of the poor and lower-middle peasants, the educated youths of the whole hsien who have gone to the countryside have achieved good health, study, and work.

3

The Placement Is Good, the Education Is Good, the Utilization Is Good

An Investigation of Chi Hsien's Good Job in Working with Educated Youths Going up to the Mountains and down to the Countryside*

Since 1964, 2,030 educated youths from Tientsin, Peking, and other cities have come to Chi hsien in Hopei Province to join the brigades and settle down. Party organizations on every level and the poor and lower-middle peasants of Chi hsien have worked hard to achieve good placement, education, and utilization of educated youths who have gone up to the mountains and down to the countryside so that they may put down roots, grow, and continually develop more active usefulness in the vast universe of the villages.

---

*Chi hsien tso-hao shang-shan hsia-hsiang chih-shih ch'ing-nien kung-tso ti tiao-ch'a. "An-chih hao, chiao-yü hao, shih-yung hao."

Careful Placement to Create Conditions for
Educated Youths to Put Down Roots in the Villages

"Chairman Mao handed educated youths to us poor and lower-
middle peasants. We had better have greater regard for them
than even for our own children and be wholeheartedly concerned." This moving statement was made by the Party branch
secretary Chang Shou-ts'ai of Chien-niu-kung Brigade, Tung-
ch'ao ko-chuang Commune. Today it has spread to every corner
of Chi hsien.

In 1969, five educated youths from Tientsin arrived at Chien-
niu-kung Brigade to join the brigade and settle down. The poor
and lower-middle peasants greeted them as though welcoming
back their own children; they had made careful preparations
for them: they raised houses, bricked in pig pens, and even
thought of crocks for salty vegetables and sacks for food, so
that the educated youths upon arrival could enter the houses and
begin cooking and go out to the fields and begin laboring. Secretary Chang Shou-ts'ai of the brigade Party branch, who had
suffered much class bitterness in the old society, was especially concerned about the educated youths, and he frequently went
to the homes of educated youths to inquire about their living
conditions. On December 29, 1970, he returned from a meeting
at the hsien with other cadres from the brigade. Even before
entering his own home, he went to look in on the educated
youths. When he saw that the educated youths had not finished
preparing their things for the New Year's festivities, he felt
badly about it. He felt that he had not done his work well, so
he immediately called the cadres to a meeting to propagate
Chairman Mao's directive on doing a good job of working with
educated youths who go up to the mountains and down to the
countryside, and he asked everyone to treat educated youths with
"even greater regard than for our own children and be wholeheartedly concerned." Under the leadership of the old Party
secretary, everyone immediately helped the educated youths
prepare things for the New Year, so that the educated youths
and the poor and lower-middle peasants together happily cele-

brated the Spring Festival in a revolutionary way. Immediately
after the Spring Festival he deputed the branch deputy secretary
to escort the educated youths back to Tientsin to visit their parents. This branch deputy secretary, house by house, home by
home, reported to the parents the many different ways in which
their children were growing in the villages. On the fifteenth,
Chang Shou-ts'ai again took the car, and braving the cold winds
and heavy snow went to the railroad station to bring these young
people back to the brigade. In the past several years, under the
tutelage of the Party and the concern of the poor and lower-
middle peasants, these young people have grown to deeply love
the village, and have grown swiftly in the Three Great Revolutionary Movements of the village. With the addition of two
youths who joined this brigade in 1970, all seven young people
have joined the League, and among them two young persons
have gloriously joined the Chinese Communist Party.

Chi hsien's hsien committee has learned from the experience
of Chien-niu-kung brigade that to do a good job of managing and
educating educated youths who have gone up to the mountains
and down to the countryside it is necessary to place them well.
It is necessary to be concerned about their living, to actively
create conditions for them to settle in the villages to carry out
the revolution. Thus, the hsien committee used the progressive
experiences of Chien-niu-kung brigade to teach the cadres and
masses of the entire hsien, calling on the responsible persons
at every level of the Party organization, and on the poor and
lower-middle peasants of the entire hsien, to be like Chang
Shou-ts'ai in his concern for the growth of educated youths.
"To regard them seriously and be wholeheartedly concerned"
has rapidly become the conscious action of cadres at every
level and of the poor and lower-middle peasants of Chi hsien.

When placing the educated youths, the hsien committees of
Chi hsien and every level of the Party organization conscientiously attended to every concrete problem. Chief among these
were:

1) The problem of housing. In the beginning, some cadres
and masses thought that the educated youths would not stay long

in the villages, that they would be there no more than three
years or so for reeducation, and that temporary living quarters
would be all right. For this reason, some communes and brigades did not grasp firmly the problem of finding housing for
educated youths settling in the countryside. When Chairman
Mao's directive on the movement of youth up to the mountains
and down to the countryside filtered down, everybody came to
understand that the movement was not a "temporary thing," but
was a great socialist revolution, a long-range plan for the cultivation and creation of tens of millions of successors to the proletarian revolution. In this way, the Party organization on every
level in Chi hsien decided to motivate the masses of poor and
lower-middle peasants, and with a spirit of self-reliance, take
appropriate measures to help the educated youths prepare materials to build houses and then help them build them. While
building, they looked to the future and built housing sufficient
for today, and sufficient also for the future when the educated
youths would have families. At present, the entire hsien has
built for the educated youths who collectively joined the brigade
1,189 rooms, averaging 0.8 rooms per person. Thus when the
educated youths marry, each family can have a living area of
one-and-a-half rooms, generally equivalent to the average living
space of the local commune members. The new houses built
for the educated youths are mostly brick, with glass and tile.
Some brigades also built pig pens and garden walls for the educated youths.

2) The problem of self-sufficiency. The hsien committee of
Chi hsien opportunely summed up and propagated the experience
of Tung-shih-ku Commune in order to solve the problem of
livelihood for the educated youths who have gone up to the
mountains and down to the countryside. Most of the educated
youths in Tung-shih-ku Commune in 1970 were not able to support themselves. They were dissatisfied, their parents were
worried, and the poor and lower-middle peasants were un-
sympathetic. The Party committee of the commune was very
concerned, and it organized a special investigatory group which
discovered three main reasons why educated youths in the

countryside were unable to realize self-sufficiency: Their work attendance was low; the educated youths, on the average, reported for work on two hundred days or so, about one-third less frequently than the local commune members. The compensation was not just; on the average the male educated youths were about two points lower than local commune members, and the female educated youths more than one point lower. They had only a single economic source and no auxiliary income.

In response to these problems revealed by the investigation, the commune Party committee adopted measures to solve them. First, they strengthened education in enthusiasm for work, so that the educated youths would strengthen their attitude toward labor. Thereafter their work attendance increased yearly. Now the average educated youth is already close to the labor level of local commune members. They also helped educated youths set up collective auxiliary projects like raising pigs, ducks, and rabbits, planting vegetables, and setting up collective dining rooms. At the same time, they educated them in economizing their ways of living and changing their wasteful attitude of "a kitchenful of firewood, a potful of rice." After these measures were taken, most of the educated youths in the commune had surplus grain, and had raised their standards of living, which made them feel secure. They became more industrious in their work and developed into very useful persons.

After the hsien committee of Chi hsien spread the experiences of Tung-shih-ku Commune, the situation of educated youths in the countryside who had been unable to support themselves continually improved through the solicitude of the Party organization at every level and the hard work of the educated youths themselves.

3) The hsien committee of Chi hsien and the Party organization at every level are also very concerned about the question of marriage for the educated youths in the countryside.

The Party organization on every level of Chi hsien and the poor and lower-middle peasants, through innumerable plans, help the educated youths in the countryside to solve real questions encountered in life. Their concern with their growth

makes the educated youths in the countryside and their parents
very satisfied.

Enthusiastic Education to Ceaselessly Raise Ideological Consciousness

The Yu-ku-chuang Brigade of Yu-ku-chuang Commune in this
hsien accepted eight educated youths to the countryside in 1969.
In the beginning, the educated youths were very enthusiastic;
their spirits were high and they wanted to accomplish something
in the construction of new socialist villages. The Party branch
of the brigade paid close attention to the placement of these educated youths and on their behalf built a six-room brick house,
put up garden walls, built a pig pen, and assigned them a vegetable garden. The implements for production and living were
also quite adequate. However, because they only concentrated
on settlement, they neglected ideological education, with the result
that some educated youths were still insufficiently adjusted to
settlement in the villages. In response to this problem, the
commune Party committee secretary Sung Lien-sheng, together
with cadres specially responsible for the settlement of educated
youths and with the Party branch of the brigade, held many study
classes for the educated youths to help them to raise their understanding.

After this study, the educated youths made encouraging progress. In 1972 each person worked an average of 269 days, 64
days more than in 1971. At the same time, some of them un-
dertook jobs as teachers, bookkeepers, agricultural technicians,
and so on. One of the educated youths in the countryside also
gloriously joined the Chinese Communist Party and was elected
a committee member of the brigade Party branch.

The hsien committee of Chi hsien saw from this event that in
order to work well with educated youths who go to the countryside, it is even more important to strengthen their ideological
and political education than to place them well, so that they will
make great strides in following the revolutionary line of Chairman Mao. Thus, under the leadership of the hsien committee,

42204

the Party organization on every level of the entire <u>hsien</u> placed educated youth work on their agenda. They strengthened and enlarged the "three-in-one" management and education groups so as to strengthen in every way the ideological and political education of educated youths.

1) They organized the educated youths to study earnestly books by Marx and Lenin and books by Chairman Mao, to criticize deeply revisionism, and to reconstruct painstakingly their worldview. This <u>hsien</u> set up or improved the study system everywhere. In addition to learning together with the masses, educated youths spent, on the average, a half day every week studying by themselves. The <u>hsien</u> and communes also, at specified times, called meetings for the educated youths to exchange study experiences.

2) Class education is a main subject. They adopted the method of inviting old, poor peasants to describe the bitterness of the past and the sweetness of the present to the educated youths; organized educated youths to view exhibits on class education, to visit the monuments to dead revolutionary heroes and other types of education in order to advance class education and education in revolutionary heritage so that they would understand the hardships of the old society and the sweetness of the new society and would forever walk on the bright road uniting with the workers and the peasants pointed out by Chairman Mao.

3) They extensively advanced education on ideals and the future. In response to the restlessness of some educated youths in the villages, and their inability to think correctly about the needs of the revolution, they organized discussions on "the ideals and future of youth" and on "putting down roots in the villages for a lifetime or for a brief while." The Party organization on every level of the <u>hsien</u> also emphasized introducing the educated youths to the enormous changes that have taken place in the villages, the flying speed in the development of production, the progress of mechanization in agriculture, so that the educated youths might see the beautiful prospect of the villages and make firm their resolution to give their youth to the new socialist villages.

4) They initiated activities for learning from progressive models. In those years, every hsien earnestly organized the educated youths to learn from the advanced examples of groups of educated youths in the brigades of this hsien such as Liu-li-t'un, Fan-chuang-tzu, Chien-niu-kung, Kuo-chuang-tzu and others, and learn from the advanced examples of educated youths in the countryside such as Kao Pao-feng, Chang Kuai-jung and others, so that among the educated youths in the countryside there appeared lively and spirited advancement of learning and a struggle for excellence.

5) The city and the countryside cooperated in the work of administering education to educated youths in the countryside. Every year the hsien committee of Chi hsien organizes cadres from the hsien, the communes, and the brigades to visit the parents of the educated youths and the schools and streets where they used to live and report to them on the growth of the educated youths, ask for their opinions, and obtain the cooperation of parents and society, so that together they may take up the responsibility of cultivating and educating the educated youths and thus obtain comparatively better results.

Bold Use to Promote the Role of Educated Youths in the Countryside

The hsien committee of Chi hsien also educated the Party organization on every level to actively cultivate and boldly use the educated youths in accordance with the special qualities of each, and to develop fully their special abilities, so that the educated youths feel that the villages really need them, that in the villages they may do great deeds. In this way the fruits of reeducation are further consolidated, and the educated youths have firmly implanted in them the thought of setting down roots in the villages and making revolution. At present, among the educated youths who have joined the brigades and made a home in this hsien, some have been elected into the leading groups of the hsien, communes, brigades and production teams; some have separately taken on the duties of teacher, barefoot doctor, bookkeeper, agricultural mechanic, agricultural technician, and so on. Shang-chiang Commune's Liu-li-t'un Brigade in the past was not accustomed to raising pigs; the educated youth Chang Kuei-jung volunteered to become pig keeper and raise pigs for the brigade; she modestly learned from the poor and lower-middle peasants, went three times to visit the troops in Yeh-hung-hai, conquered various types of difficulties, and made up a sweetened feeding substance. By studying intensively, she learned to treat pig illnesses, and helped to solve problems that the collective and commune members had in feeding and preventing illnesses in pigs. This brigade has already realized the goal of one pig for every person and has become an advanced unit in the hsien in pig raising. With more pigs, there is more manure and the food production has also increased. Since 1971 the yield per mou in food of this brigade has for two years continuously surpassed the "Program." Three educated youths including Kao Pao-feng, who had settled in the Fan-chuang-tzu Brigade of Yu-ku-chuang Commune which had complicated class struggles, began to waver in their thoughts and felt that they could not stay there any longer. After the Party committee of the commune discovered the sprouts of such thinking in them, it immediately carried out education with them, pushed them on to the front lines of the class struggle, supporting them in being first to remove the lid of the class struggle in that brigade and to criticize the tendency toward capitalism. Having undergone this struggle, the consciousness of line struggle of the cadres and the masses was heightened and the entire brigade very quickly showed a new spirit of grasping the revolution and promoting agriculture. The educated youths in the countryside also experienced tempering and testing. Kao Pao-feng entered the Party and was selected to be the deputy secretary of the brigade Party branch; the other two young people also separately took on the responsibilities of deputy secretary of the Youth League branch and platoon leader of the militia. They felt that the harder the place, the more they are able to temper themselves; that places where the conditions are less good particularly need them for construction. They have planted three trees in front of the house that will put down roots, and they are determined to be like those little trees and put down roots and grow in Fan-chuang-tzu.

The educated youths are a most active and most energetic force in the construction of the new socialist villages. The poor and lower-middle peasants, seeing the progress of the educated youths, are glad in their hearts, and happily say, "These children have culture, they are energetic and active. They really are good successors to the proletarian revolution."

Chi hsien Revolutionary Committee Reporting Group,
Tientsin Region Revolutionary Committee Reporting Group,
Hsin-hua reporter

4

Erh-shih-chia-tzu Commune Is Doing a Good Job
with Educated Youths Who Have Gone
down to the Countryside*

Erh-shih-chia-tzu Commune in Huai-te hsien, Chilin Province, is an advanced unit in the provincial movement to learn
from Tachai in agriculture. It is situated on the east bank of
the Liao River; half of it is mountainous, and on the average,
each person has 3.8 mou of arable land. Since 1968, 607 educated youths from Shanghai and this hsien have come to this
place to join the brigades and settle down (currently there are
345); they are organized into 23 collective households. In these
years, the commune Party committee has conscientiously im-
plemented the revolutionary line of Chairman Mao, and warmly
and wholeheartedly welcomed the educated youths, cultivating
them with all their hearts and energy. The collective households have been administered comparatively well, and the young
people have grown very quickly. Among the educated youths who
went to the countryside, 28 joined the Party; 323 joined the Youth
League; 54 joined the leadership ranks of the province, hsien,

---

*"Erh-shih-chia-tzu kung-she hsia-hsiang chih-shih ch'ing-
nien kung-tso tso-ti hao."

29

commune, and brigade; 23 took jobs as bookkeepers, teachers, barefoot doctors, custodians [pao-kuan yuan], and so on. Fourteen persons have already married in the villages. The educated youths have already become fresh reinforcements in the movement to learn from Tachai in agriculture. Of the twenty production teams which set up collective households before 1972, five in the last year have crossed the "Yellow River" [i.e., achieved self-sufficiency] in grain production and nine have surpassed the "Program." Ninety-five percent of the educated youths can take care of their own clothing, food, miscellaneous, and medical expenses with income from their own labor, and 81 percent of the young people even have surplus funds. Because the collective households were relatively well set up, this year 39 young people have followed their elder brothers and sisters here to join the brigades and make a home. The masses say: The work of educated youths has been worthy of the leaders' solicitude; the young people are at ease; the parents are not worried; and the poor and lower-middle peasants are contented.

Ceaselessly Raise Understanding, and Let the Revolutionary Line of Chairman Mao Take Root in the Leaders' Thinking

In October 1969, when a group of educated youths came to this commune to join the brigade and settle down, some of the leading members held that the educated youths had come for supplementary labor classes, that when the time came, they would leave; some held that the responsibility of learning from Tachai in agriculture was a great one, that the work of educating educated youths was a great one, that not doing it well would affect the central tasks. For these reasons, this item of work was treated as a temporary duty.

Later, the revolutionary actions of the poor and lower-middle peasants and of the educated youths educated the commune leaders. The leading comrades of the commune saw with their own eyes the poor and lower-middle peansats actively and warmly lead the educated youths in building houses, building pig pens,

digging wells and planting trees, and they said, Chairman Mao
let the young people come to the villages; we must help them
settle down and make a home. The role of educated youths in
the movement to learn from Tachai in agriculture also became
more and more apparent. The collective household which con-
stituted the No. 7 Team in Hsiao-shan Brigade, under the leadership of the Party branch, actively struggled against class
enemies and capitalistic tendencies. They carried sand and
boulders with the poor and lower-middle peasants, overcame
torrential floods, leveled land, and worked hard to change the
conditions of production; very quickly they changed from being
a "foot-dragging brigade" to being a "leaping-forward brigade."
The production of grain per mou in one year was raised from
236 chin to 502 chin, crossing over the "Yellow River." These
moving facts deeply educated the commune Party committee.
In the rectification movement to criticize revisionism, the comrades from the commune Party committee earnestly criticized
the reactionary and fallacious statements propagated by swindlers like Liu Shao-ch'i such as "study to become an official,"
"go to the countryside to get a patina of experience," and "disguised reform through labor." The commune Party committee
also carried out open meeting rectification, examined work,
summed up experiences, and looked for inadequacies in
thought. It advanced one step further in its understanding
that Chairman Mao's call for educated youths to go up to
the mountains and down to the countryside is not a temporary
measure, but is a strategy to cultivate successors to the proletarian revolutionary cause. Whether rivers and mountains
change in the future will depend on whether the young generation
can raise class struggle and line struggle, maintain revolutionary consciousness, and continue the revolutionary tradition of
the older generation. The educated youths need to come to the
villages to experience buffeting and tempering, and the new socialist villages need young people to be their "new beams and
new pillars." The class enemies obstruct the participation of
educated youths in physical labor precisely in order to struggle
with us for the younger generation. It is necessary for the vil-

lage basic-level Party committee to grasp the grain sprouts; it
is even more necessary to grasp the "human sprouts"; and it is
necessary, in the struggle between two classes for the winning
over of the youths, to resolutely defend Chairman Mao's revolutionary line. Only by allowing the revolutionary line of Chairman Mao to put down roots in one's own mind can we educate
the young people to put down roots in the villages.

Once its understanding of ideology was raised, the commune
Party committee placed the matter of educated youths on the
agenda of important matters for the Party committee, and the
Party committee secretary took the lead in working with educated youths. When the Party committee secretary, Kao Te-
ch'ing, went down to investigate local conditions, he frequently
went to the "collective households" in order to understand their
conditions; when the Party committee members meet, they frequently report on the situation of the educated youths; at meetings of cadres of the three levels*, the young household heads of
the "collective households" are asked to participate, so that they
may understand the situation, be clear as to responsibilities,
and be better able to develop their usefulness. If the young people
of the "collective households" develop problematical tendencies,
the Party committee immediately discusses them in order to
solve them. Because he frequently makes contact with the
masses of young people, the Party committee secretary knows
by name more than 80 percent of the educated youths of the entire commune, and he can understand their thinking and their
special abilities. Under the leadership of the secretary, the
Party committee members are all serious about working with
educated youths in the countryside. When distributing leadership work, they do the central work and also work with the educated youths. The deputy secretary, Li Ching-t'ai, when dividing the responsibility for the rectification campaign for criticizing revisionism, actively organized the educated youths to
participate in the criticizing-revisionism movement of the production brigade, giving the young people special tutoring in that

*See the Glossary.

subject, relating it to reality, and leading them to deal correctly with their ideals and their futures.

In order to strengthen the leadership of the groups, the commune selected and matched for every collective family a family head who is an old poor peasant, an old Party member, or an old cadre member who has had good thinking, correct action, and a plain life. They also motivated cadres of the production brigade and cadres who joined the brigade to work with educated youths. All told, they held thirty-one sessions of "old household head" study classes. These measures created a new situation in the work of educating the educated youths in the countryside in which "the Party committee secretary himself, the Party committee members individually, the commune and brigade cadres on every level, all grasped responsibility."

When the educated youths in the countryside grew quickly in their political thinking, became more settled in the villages, and showed achievements in their work, some of the leading comrades in the commune again began to relax, feeling that having special persons responsible for grasping this task was sufficient. At that time, the commune Party committee brought together some problems that had developed within the collective households of educated youths and renewed the study of the teachings of Chairman Mao in order to plant firmly the idea that one must do this work well for a long time. Then later, when some of the educated youths were selected and transferred to another front line, some comrades developed the idea that "the work of administering education is almost at an end." The commune Party committee organized everyone yet again to study the relevant teachings of Chairman Mao and to analyze earnestly the circumstances and problems of working with the educated youths in the countryside, asking that this work continue to be firmly and well grasped and raised to a new level.

Be Good at Discovering Socialist Activism
in the Basic Nature of Youth

The Party committee of Erh-shih-chia-tzu Commune, in

working with educated youths, followed the teachings of Chairman Mao and regarded the young people as a revolutionary force that is the most active, most energetic, most willing to learn and least conservative in thought. This led them to discover from their basic nature the socialist activism of the young people. They understood that:

1) It is necessary to have deep proletarian feelings. They say, "Without these feelings, it is not possible to grasp; if the feelings are not deep, the grasp is not good." In the No. 4 Team of Hsi-ti Brigade, the old poor peasant Liu Sheng, who is the head of the collective household and a Party member, carefully looked after the young people, personally taught them to work, and frequently talked to the young people about his family history and the village history, helping them to progress politically, and aiding them to take action and do things courageously. The youth Wang Heng-chen once swept up the beans that had fallen on the ground to feed to the pigs, but Liu Sheng took the dust bin from him and picked out the beans one by one, teaching Wang Heng-chen to economize on food. Later, Wang Heng-chen became the custodian and was very protective of the food. Under the careful cultivation of Liu Sheng, the thirteen young people of the household all progressed very quickly; four joined the Party, five joined the League, and three joined leadership groups. Comrade Liu Sheng often says, "They listened to the words of Chairman Mao and are making revolution accordingly; we should care for them as we care for our sons who are in the military."

2) Class education is a main subject. The educated youths lack experience in class struggle. The commune Party committee takes every group of educated youths who arrive here to the manor of the former landlord and asks the old poor peasants who had worked for the landlord to talk about the village history and their family history; they take them to heroes' graves and ask old revolutionary soldiers to talk about the revolutionary tradition and the history of the revolutionary war. They have also organized the youths to investigate the history and the current situation of class struggle and line struggle in

the production team from land reform to the Cultural Revolution. They summarize these activities and organize the young people to study the great sayings of Chairman Mao concerning class, class contradictions, and class struggle, in order to strengthen their concept of class struggle. A youth born in a family of the old exploiting class was digging a well one winter day when a rich peasant said to her, "On such a cold day, if you were in the city, you might be sitting in the late showing of a movie!" She immediately realized that this was a class enemy's rash plan to confuse people's hearts, and right then and there, with the other youths, she criticized and struggled with this rich peasant. At present the educated youths at this commune have already become active in developing all types of political activities. Much attention has been given to discovering elements of activism in the few backward youths and raising their class consciousness through deep and detailed ideological work, helping them conquer their mistakes and weaknesses with fervor and enthusiasm, and pointing out the direction of progress.

3) Teach and promote the positive role of educated youth in the countryside in the Three Great Revolutionary Struggles. The commune Party committee realizes that it cannot treat young people like someone flying a kite, who wants to fly it high, but is afraid of breaking the string. They always put youths in the front lines of the Three Great Revolutionary Struggles so that they may consciously restructure their subjective world while restructuring the objective world. Erh-shih-chia-tzu Brigade's No. 6 Team has 75 mou of "red sand and gravel" land, the produce from each mou being but 100 chin. The collective household from this brigade suggested reconstructing this piece of thin land. The Party committee members who were visiting there actively supported their suggestion. The educated youths from this household each took a set of shoulder poles, and together with the poor and lower-middle peasants, carried soil to this piece of land; altogether 1,450 tons of black soil were carried, changing the "red sand and gravel" to fertile land and good fields. The production per mou crossed the "Yellow River." In order to achieve high production, the commune decided

to allow the collective household of the No. 3 Team of Hsiao-shan
Brigade to carry out scientific experiments with close planting
of pao rice. In 1970 the ten-odd educated youths from this
household carried out the experiment of "close-planting three
seeds in one mound." On the average the production per mou
was more than 1,000 chin. The next year, this was carried out throughout the entire commune, and the surface area
production of each unit was greatly raised. Lui Kuei-hsi, an
educated youth in Chuan-chieh Brigade, worked hard studying
the works of Chairman Mao, actively participated in the collective production movement, and progressed very quickly, becoming the vice chairman of the brigade revolutionary committee. In order to let him increase his abilities through practice,
the Party branch sent him to visit the No. 3 Team and the No. 5
Team, where the class struggle was more complicated, and also
sent an old cadre to be his "consultant." Liu Kuei-hsi emphasized investigation and research, relied on the masses, and very
quickly removed the lid of class struggle in these two teams.
He attacked class enemies, criticized capitalistic tendencies,
advanced the unity of the leading group, so that the appearance
of these two brigades developed noticeable changes that year.

Arrange the Living Appropriately,
Create Conditions for Educated Youths to
Put Down Roots in the Villages

The Erh-shih-chia-tzu Commune Party committee has always
regarded good living arrangements for educated youths as a
minimal condition for contented participation in the construction
of new villages, and as an important factor for thoroughly carrying out the revolutionary line of Chairman Mao. Even though
most of the educated youths in the countryside of this commune
are more than self-sufficient, the commune Party committee
still concerns itself several times each year with the question
of the educated youths' living conditions. They are concerned
with each household and with solving every problem. When
spring arrives, they attend to making soy sauce, planting vege-

tables, and cleaning house; when autumn comes, they clean out
the store, collect firewood, and cook food. The Hsi-ti No. 2
Team's collective household at first had no plans for regulating
the use of their food; so the Party committee deputy secretary,
Tan Kuei-hsiang, taught them how to plan the use of food and
personally helped them to set up a plan for using food. The
No. 1 Team of Kao Tai-tzu Brigade has educated youths from
Shanghai, who when they first came to the village did not know
how to plant vegetables, so the team Party branch went to a
neighboring vegetable team to ask two old peasants to come and
teach them how to plant vegetables. Each and every production
team arranged for youths who are physically weak to join in labor appropriate to their strength, such as herding pigs, herding
cows, looking after the children, gathering and storing fertilizer,
and so on. In order to look after the special physiology of the
girls, some families even selected poor and lower-middle wom-
en peasants as household heads. The Party committee personally lead each office in looking after all aspects of the livelihood
of the educated youths.

In solving the problems of livelihood of the educated youths
in the countryside, they emphasized the correct disposition of
the following three related matters:

1) Livelihood and production: Production is the basis of livelihood. Therefore they motivated the educated youths in the
countryside to actively participate in the mass movement to
learn from Tachai in agriculture, struggle hard, carry out the
basic construction of agricultural fields, and carry out scientific
planting on a large scale to change the appearance of the production team. With the concerted hard work of the poor and
lower-middle peasants and the educated youths in the countryside, the food production of the entire commune has increased each
year. In 1965 the total production was 5,500 tons (till then the
greatest production in several years); in 1972, although there
were severe natural disasters, it still doubled, reaching 11,400
tons. Following the development of collective production, the
individual income of educated youths also increased; on the average each person's income in 1970 was 186 yuan; in 1971,

262 yuan; and in 1972, 255 yuan.

2) Putting one's hands out or putting one's hands to work:
Teach the educated youths that the foundation for an abundance
of clothing and food is constructed by their own efforts. They
must actively participate in productive labor, support the family
through frugality, and rely on their own strength to solve the
livelihood problems of the collective household. Under the tutelage of the Party, the work attendance of the educated youths in
this commune increases each year; the boys and girls on the
average each reported for work 225 days in 1970, 245 days in
1971, and 267 days in 1972. The collective household of the
No. 2 Team of Nan-shan Brigade suggested using the living
expenses to go to the city to buy coal when they first arrived in
the village. The old household head, Li Pin-ch'en, taught the
young people, "We are half mountains around here, firewood
and grass are all over the mountains, how can you buy coal?"
Under the leadership of the old household head, the young people
went up the mountains to collect firewood, and in seven days they
collected enough firewood for the collective household to use for
half a year. The commune Party committee propagated their
experience; later many of the collective households did things
for themselves, from raising little chickens and making soy
sauce to making bricks, repairing the store, and maintaining
their living quarters. The commune's twenty-three collective
households depended on self-sufficiency, working hard and
struggling, and have basically achieved economy in food, self-
sufficiency in oil, meat, and eggs, and surplus in vegetables.

3) The present and the future: Grasp firmly the basic construction of the collective household both by starting from present needs and also by long-range planning. When the collective
households were building houses, the commune and brigade cadres personally helped pick out sites for the houses, coordinating
them with the houses of commune members in every production
team. The houses were spacious, bright, and practical, so that
living, eating, and storing things were all very convenient.
Every family had a storage granary. In eighteen collective
households, ping pong tables were set up, which serve as dining

tables and study tables as well as ping pong tables. Each collective household raises pigs and chickens, some even raise rabbits, and all have garden plots. Some households have created woods, planted fruit trees, and harvested grapes; fifteen households have dug their own wells. The collective households of the No. 1 Team of Hou-shih Brigade planted more than thirty mou of pine forest and also planted fruit trees.

In the past few years, because the Erh-shih-chia-tzu Commune Party committee comprehensively and thoroughly carried out the directives and policies of Chairman Mao and the Central Committee of the Party concerning educated youths going up to the mountains and down to the countryside, unceasingly summed up experiences, and raised the conscious implementation of Chairman Mao's revolutionary line, the work is carried out better and better. The masses of educated youths in the countryside feel warm in their politics, happy in their work, and satisfied in their lives, so that they increasingly love the villages and have become fresh reinforcements for the construction of new socialist villages.

CCP Chilin Provincial Committee, Huai-te Hsien Committee Investigation Group

5

Hung-ch'i Brigade Is Concerned about All Aspects of
the Growth of Educated Youths Who Have Gone
down to the Countryside*

Hung-ch'i Brigade of P'ing-kang Commune in Huo-ch'iu hsien,
Anhwei, is an advanced unit for doing good work with educated
youths in the countryside. This brigade, since 1969, has welcomed fifty-three educated youths to the countryside. In more
than four years since then these educated youths, under the tutelage of the Party organizations and the poor and lower-middle
peasants, have been tempered in the Three Great Revolutionary
Movements of the villages. They have become good aides when
the cadres and masses read and study, daring little generals in
class struggle, attackers in the production struggle, and red
vanguard soldiers in scientific experimentation. In the process
of mutually uniting with the poor and lower-middle peasants,
their thinking and their emotions have deeply changed: those
who in the past did not want to go to the villages now love the
villages; those who in the past did not have deep feelings concerning the poor and lower-middle peasants now feel that the
poor and lower-middle peasants are very close. The cadres

---

*"Hung-ch'i ta-tui ch'uan-mien kuan-huai hsia-hsiang chih-
shih ch'ing-nien ti-ch'eng-chang."

40

and masses of Hung-ch'i Brigade educated the educated youths, but they also learned many things from the young people; they especially learned that the young people are vigorous and enthusiastic, are the most willing to learn, have the least conservative thinking, have a revolutionary spirit of daring to think and daring to do, enabling the cadres and masses to make very great progress. The cadres and masses of Hung-ch'i Brigade, whenever speaking of the educated youths, become exceedingly excited, praising ceaselessly.

In these years, because the educated youths in the countryside and the poor and lower-middle peasants have fought heaven and earth together to achieve rich harvests and speed up the pace of the movement to learn from Tachai in agriculture, the production picture of the entire brigade has changed greatly. Hung-ch'i Brigade was originally a regressive brigade that "needed goods and money, needed help, and needed grain furnished," producing in 1968 only a little over 300 chin of grain per mou. After the educated youths arrived in the countryside, they received reeducation, and they worked with the poor and lower-middle peasants digging ditches and channels, regulating the mountains and the water, and developing many different scientific research activities such as comparing different strains of aquatic rice, transplanting cotton, cultivating green manure, experimentally growing mushroom fertilizer, improving agricultural implements, and so on, thus reaping a noticeable increase in production. In 1971, the production of grain per mou met the quota; in 1972, the grain quota was exceeded by 1,000 chin, the pig-raising quota was exceeded, and many other types of operations showed great development. In four years, more than a million chin of grain was contributed to the state. These are the initial accomplishments of fifty-three educated youths working shoulder to shoulder with the poor and lower-middle peasants and the masses of the commune.

Because work with educated youths in the countryside was carried out well, the "three satisfactions" [san-man-i] have appeared. The first is that the poor and lower-middle peasants are satisfied. Since the arrival of the educated youths in the countryside, the entire brigade has experienced a series of changes, and the attitude of the masses of cadres and people toward the educated youths has also begun to change correspondingly. The team leader of Ta-pei Production Team, Chu Pang-kuo, originally felt that the arrival of the educated youths was a burden and he did not want it; in 1970, two educated youths arrived and proved useful in many ways; having tasted the initial sweetness of it, he now clamors for more. In the past, afraid that they would come, now, afraid that they will go; reality has changed the attitudes of some people toward the educated youths. The two production brigades, Ta-t'ang and Chien-tan, had educated youths who were absorbed into factories when it came time to recruit labor, and the production team leader was loathe to have them go. The poor and lower-middle peasants said: "From now on, if an educated youth goes, we must have another educated youth sent here."

The second is that the educated youths are satisfied. The educated youths, under the warm and concerned tutelage of the brigade Party organization and the poor and lower-middle peasants, have their eating, living, daily needs, etc., all arranged very well, and they are progressing very fast in their political thinking and productive labor, so that they feel satisfied and have come to love this place. Some of the educated youths who have been recruited to work in factories do not want to go and, once they have gone, frequently come back here "to visit relatives." An educated youth from Shanghai was selected last year to go to Liu-an to study in an instructor's class; during summer vacations, he returns to the brigade to join in productive labor; during winter vacations, he returns here to pass the Spring Festival. The educated youths all treat Hung-ch'i Brigade as their own home. Some of the educated youths plan to ask their younger brothers and sisters to come here to join the brigade and settle down when they have graduated.

The third is that the parents are satisfied. We see letter after letter from the parents of the educated youths, each one filled with warmth, thanking the brigade Party branch and the poor and lower-middle peasants for their concern for and the education and cultivation of their sons and daughters. The great changes in Hung-ch'i Brigade in the past few years have deeply touched and attracted the parents of the educated youths. At present, already eleven of the educated youths' parents and family members have taken the initiative to move the whole family from the city to this place to settle down.

Why is the work of the educated youths done so well at Hung-ch'i Brigade? Their main experiences are:

Resolutely Implement the Revolutionary Line of Chairman Mao

How should educated youths be treated? How should we regard this great revolution of educated youths going up to the mountains and down to the countryside? On this question, there is a fierce struggle of two kinds of thought, two classes, and two lines. Hung-ch'i Brigade's good work with educated youths in the countryside has its key point in the Party branch's resolute implementation of Chairman Mao's revolutionary line and in the cadres' and masses' correct understanding of educated youths in the countryside.

In Hung-ch'i Brigade, everyone, whether a cadre from the brigade or from a production team, or a poor and lower-middle peasant, firmly remembers the great teaching of Chairman Mao that "educated youths must go to the villages to receive reeducation from the poor and lower-middle peasants.... Comrades from villages everywhere should welcome their going," and regard the work of receiving, settling, administering, and educating educated youths as an important matter in implementing the revolutionary line of Chairman Mao. They understand that the movement of educated youths up to the mountains and down to the countryside is a great socialist revolution, a great strategic measure in the cultivation and creation of successors to the proletarian revolution, and a necessity for the construction of new socialist villages. Sending educated youths to the villages, entrusting them to the poor and lower-middle peasants, and bidding the poor and lower-middle peasants to take up the heavy

burden of their cultivation and education demonstrates the great
trust and concern for the poor and lower-middle peasants by
Chairman Mao and other elders. The educated youths have
come, and the villages are more prosperous. Therefore, everyone has extremely strong feelings of glory and of responsibility.
They say, "We must not fail to live up to the expectations of
Chairman Mao and other elders; we must lead the youths properly so that the elders will be at ease." Thus their love for the
educated youths is deep, and their reeducation work with the
educated youths is thought out well and carried out with care.
The entire brigade on every level is of one heart; everybody
lends a hand and together shoulders this subsidiary responsibility. On discovering that a young person is upset, they will
become anxious, feeling that they have not done their utmost in
their responsibilities; on seeing that some young people still
cannot be self-sufficient in their living and ask for money from
home, they will become worried; on seeing that more parents
are sending letters, and fewer parents are sending money and
bringing things, they feel that the parents have become relaxed
about their children's lives in the villages. Then they are happy. Because the cadres and masses of the brigade have this
kind of deep proletarian feeling, year by year, month by month,
and day by day they concern themselves with the growth of the
educated youths who have come to the countryside.

The cadres and poor and lower-middle peasants of Hung-ch'i
Brigade, in their personal emotions, have come to understand
deeply that they cannot do without educated youths in the construction of new socialist villages. Thus, they regard the educated youths as a precious treasure. This further stimulates
their activism in working well with educated youths in the countryside. Of course, this understanding also came about through
a process. In the beginning, some people, seeing that when educated youths first came to the villages they could not do this and
did not understand that, and some times were not even very attentive, regarded the educated youths as a "burden." However,
they very quickly felt that this kind of attitude was not right.
With deep feeling they say that, as Chairman Mao has pointed

out, "the young people are the most active, most energetic force
in the whole society." So long as we have a warm concern, patiently educate them, and do our work thoroughly, we can fully
motivate their activism, so that they may conquer those weaknesses that lie in the path of advancement, healthily grow in the
struggles of the Three Great Revolutions of the villages, and
develop greater and greater usefulness. When people ask the
cadres and poor and lower-middle peasants of this brigade
whether "the educated youths' coming to the brigade have caused
you to worry," they always say, "In the beginning, we worried a
little, but this was worrying for the revolution, it is an honor;
now they are already our good consultants and worry together
with us about constructing new socialist villages."

Conscientiously Do Good Educational Administration Work

The Hung-ch'i Brigade Party branch, responding to the characteristic of educated youths in the countryside to regress in
their ideology, adopted some good methods for administering
education. They have conscientiously and carefully done good
work on the basis of "serious attention by the leadership, concern by all poor and lower-middle peasants and by cadres,
striving for cooperation of the parents, and having the old guide
the new."

1) Serious Attention by the Leadership. The brigade set up
a leadership group, with the brigade Party branch deputy secretary Chu Pang-yü specifically responsible. Each branch member separately cooperated in the ideological education of the
educated youths. Each production team also had a special person responsible. The Party branch committee held a meeting
every month to study the thinking of the educated youths and, if
there were problems, immediately set out to solve them. The
cadres and the poor and lower-middle peasants frequently emphasize praising the good persons and good works among the
educated youths, encouraging them to improve. Every week
the young people are organized to hold political study, and at
the end of every year there is an evaluation session with the

educated youths. At the same time, the Party branch members
frequently go among the educated youths to discuss their feelings and do ideological work. The leading cadres of the brigade
always are the first to visit the educated youths when they return from outside meetings. Once, the brigade Party branch
secretary, Sun Hsiu-fa, found that the educated youth Hsiao
Hsüeh had become gloomy and silent after visiting her family
in Shanghai, so he immediately sought her out to discuss her
feelings, and discovered that Hsiao Hsüeh had heard some idle
talk and rumors in Shanghai which had affected her thinking.
He immediately educated her concerning ideals and the future,
helping her to establish the idea of setting down roots in the
villages to carry out the revolution.

2) Concern by All Poor and Lower-Middle Peasants and by
Cadres. The brigade Party branch deeply understands that
work with educated youths, like other work, requires taking the
mass line and depends on the participation of everyone before
it can work well. In the past several years, the Party branch
members have set an example and have actively done good work
with educated youths, and in addition they have repeatedly mobilized the masses of poor and lower-middle peasants to voluntarily shoulder this subsidiary heavy burden. Right now, each
of the poor and lower-middle peasants of the brigade is concerning himself about the educated youths, each is working with
the educated youths. Each day, if an educated youth does not
come to work, everyone will sympathetically ask after them. If
some young girl who likes to talk and laugh goes about her work
without a sound, they feel that there is some problem and hasten
to help her solve it. Once, three educated girls from Ta-pa
Production Team threw away the salted vegetables that the poor
and lower-middle peasants had given them; when a poor peasant,
Aunty Ch'en, saw this, she invited them to her home and inviting them to a meal for recalling hardship; she seriously and
sincerely educated them not to forget past bitterness while living in comfort, thus giving these youths a vivid class education.

The cadres in the brigade who were sent to the countryside
[hsia-fang] are also concerned about the growth of the educated

youths. Ever since hsia-fang cadre Chang Pu-jan arrived here
in 1970, he has frequently gone among the educated youths, and
using his personal understanding derived from his own acceptance of reeducation, he has helped the educated youths raise
their conscious acceptance of reeducation. He often takes
the opportunity when he is on official business or doing work in
the city to buy political and cultural study materials for the educated youths, and sometimes he even gives political and cultural classes for the educated youths. If the educated youths
become sick, he is busy asking the doctors to come, fetching
medicine, and asking after their comfort. The educated youths
are moved and say, "Old Chang is more concerned about us than
about himself! "

3) Cooperation of the Parents of Educated Youths Is Sought.
The Hung-ch'i Brigade Party branch has used a great many different methods to maintain close relationships with the parents
of the educated youths, striving for their cooperation so that,
together, they can do a good job with educated youths. For those educated youths whose parents live in local towns and cities, the
cadres make use of the opportunity when they are in town for
meetings or business to visit the families and report to the parents the condition of the educated youths in the villages, ex-
changing views with them, advancing the understanding of the
concrete situation of every educated youth, so that upon return
work can be carried out on target. For the educated youths
whose families live in Shanghai, they chiefly maintain relationships with the parents through letters. Besides this, every year
they insist on sending an evaluation of the educated youths to the
parents, so that the parents may comprehensively understand
the situation of their children in the villages that year in terms
of tempering and growth, and can cooperate in doing good education work.

4) The Old Are Used to Guide the New. The Hung-ch'i Brigade Party committee has learned from its practical work that
mobilizing the educated youths who arrived earlier to work with
newly arrived educated youths and using the old to lead the new
for mutual advance is a fruitful method of carrying out work.

In 1968, the brigade received a group of educated youths. After that, every time a new group of educated youths arrived, the Party branch always selected a few educated youths who had arrived earlier to be with them, teach them how to organize their lives, and introduce them to the situation so that they may become used to the new environment as quickly as possible. The Party branch has also held discussion groups with the educated youths, so that the educated youths who arrived earlier can discuss their thinking and their learning, inspiring the new comrades-in-arms to set down roots in the villages, to receive reeducation better, and to develop a useful role in the villages. Ta-pa Production Team has a few female educated youths from Shanghai who, when they first came, did not know how to cook, so the Party branch sent educated youth Tsao Ch'eng-fang who had come earlier to teach them how to cook and help them to set up their study plans.

The Hung-ch'i Brigade Party branch, in the course of working with educated youths in the countryside, has emphasized grasping the following items of work:

1) Mobilize the Educated Youths to Participate in the Movement to Learn from Tachai in Agriculture and Develop Agricultural Production. The brigade Party branch realizes that in working with educated youths one cannot be satisfied with simply getting them settled well, but should also get them to be content to set down roots in the villages to carry out revolution for a lifetime. To achieve this goal, besides doing a good job of ideological education, it is also necessary to mobilize the educated youths in the countryside to work together with the poor and lower-middle peasants to develop the movement to learn from Tachai in agriculture, and work hard at developing agricultural production. They say, "We want to work together with the educated youths to make Hung-ch'i Brigade a good place in every way so that the young people will feel that there are some prospects in the villages, and in their hearts will come to love the villages." For this reason, in settlement work they have always emphasized developing agricultural production. In 1969, the Party branch, together with the poor and lower-middle peasants

and the educated youths, set up the construction plans for Hung-
ch'i Brigade. After that, with every group of educated youths
that came, the brigade cadres would first take them to the highest point in the brigade, the crow's stone watchtower, and talk
to them about the long-range plans of the brigade, so that the
youths from the beginning would establish a goal to struggle for.
In these four years, the Party branch has guided the poor and
lower-middle peasants, the masses of commune members, and
the educated youths to work hard and truly learn from Tachai,
to do basic agricultural construction, and to carry out scientific
planting. As a result there were great changes in the production picture. After a few years of hard work, the production volume greatly increased. The swift development of production not only set up the material conditions for the settling
of educated youths, but also caused the educated youths to learn
from the change in the brigade about the beautiful future of the
new socialist villages and to deeply feel that the villages con-
tain good prospects and a good future and thus to be even more
able to carry out revolution in the villages without anxiety.

2) Fully Develop the Usefulness of the Educated Youths in
the Villages. The Party branch not only takes seriously the
work of educating the educated youths, but also emphasizes the
bold use of the educated youths and the full development of their
usefulness. They know this: good reeducation work enables the
educated youths to grow quickly and healthily and to develop
their usefulness. The process of utilizing them is also a process of reeducating them. Only by boldly using them and, while
using them, resolutely carrying out education can they most
quickly increase their abilities. On the basis of this knowledge,
in the past few years they have resolutely given the educated
youths work, given them responsibility, let them shoulder a
heavy burden, so that they could use their abilities to the utmost. In these four years, the brigade Party branch has received three educated youths as Party members and has elected
them to join the leadership ranks of the Party branch; among
these, two have been deputy secretaries in the Party branch.
Three educated youths became deputy chairmen of the brigade

revolutionary committee, deputy secretary of the League branch, and deputy battalion commander of the militia. Three educated youths have become deputy brigade leaders of the production brigades. There was also a group of educated youths who became bookkeepers for the production brigades, timekeepers, tractor operators, teachers in popularly managed schools, barefoot doctors, agricultural technicians, and so on. Besides this, scientific experimentation groups, literature and art propaganda groups, and information and reporting groups were set up based on the special characteristics and skills of each youth, so that each and every person has a responsibility. The educated youth Huang Ch'ing-hsiang, after he joined the leadership ranks of the production team, was totally concerned about how to do the work of the production team well. When he saw some differences between the team leader and the deputy team leader, he was very anxious. He understood that the two brigade leaders had worked together and begged together, and after liberation entered the Party together and became team cadres, so he began to write the family history for them both. When he went to the team leader's home to write the family history, he invited the deputy brigade leader to come also and recall the past; when he read the family history for the deputy brigade leader, he invited the brigade leader to sit in and listen. After this remembrance of past bitterness and thinking of present sweetness, the two brigade leaders raised their consciousness, eliminated the gap between them, and strengthened their unity.

3) Raise the Level of the Political Thinking and the Cultural and Scientific Level of the Educated Youths in the Countryside to Meet the Needs of the Village in the Three Great Revolutionary Struggles. In our concern for the growth of educated youths, we must first strengthen their education in political thought and help them experience the winds and rains and learn about the world in the Three Great Revolutionary Struggles. At the same time, they must be helped to raise their knowledge of culture and science, and unceasingly advance along the road of "both red and expert" in order to meet the daily increasing needs of the socialist revolution construction work.

In the Three Great Revolutionary Movements in the villages,
the brigade Party branch discovered that the book knowledge
which the educated youths had formerly learned in the schools
was already inadequate. Thus they organized them to study political theory conscientiously, participate actively in the Three
Great Revolutionary Struggles, and also set aside a definite
amount of time to study culture, so that they may raise their
cultural and scientific knowledge and develop their usefulness
in the villages. Last May, the brigade formally organized an
educated youth spare-time school, setting up classes in four
subjects — politics, language, mathematics, and agricultural
techniques. Based on the special attributes of the villages,
classes were held together, and discussions were held in small
groups; able people were the teachers, and everyone taught and
learned from each other. Every week there was a day for collective study, which counted as a half-day work point. In this
way, the educated youths have not only consolidated the textbook
knowledge learned in the past in schools, but also raised their
political consciousness, learned quite a lot of new cultural and
scientific knowledge, and grown in capability.

Show Warm Concern for the Lives of the Educated Youths

The Hung-ch'i Brigade Party branch has done a good job with
educated youths in the countryside by emphasizing a warm concern for every aspect of their lives. They understand that concern about the livelihood of educated youths is an important
guarantee in urging educated youths to put down roots in the
villages and carry out revolution.

1) Conscientiously Do a Good Job of Settlement. The brigade
built for every small group which joined the brigade a solid,
practical, and roomy house, and a kitchen, bathroom, pig pen,
and so on. The sites for the houses were selected to be close
to where the cadres and the poor and lower-middle peasants
lived, so that looking after them would be convenient. Every
small group which joined the brigade was completely set up
with the implements needed in daily life and with production

tools. In the autumn of 1971, the brigade again received nineteen educated youths from Shanghai. In order for them to settle in the new houses as soon as possible, a few families of poor and lower-middle peasants volunteered to stop construction on houses which they were building for themselves and use their collective strength to complete construction on the houses of the educated youths first.

2) Help the Educated Youths Realize Self-Sufficiency. The Party branch frequently teaches the educated youths to be like the poor and lower-middle peasants, not fearing hardship, or fatigue, actively participating in collective production labor, and at the same time helping them set up systems in labor checks, vacation requests, and so on. Last year the educated youths of the entire brigade averaged more than 280 days of work attendance, and the majority reached 324 days.

In order to help the educated youths quickly grasp the skills of production and come up to par in work points, the masses of commune members have been motivated to educate them at all times and all places, and every production brigade has selected an old poor peasant with the most production experience to be responsible for teaching production skills to the educated youths. At present, following the policy of equal pay for equal work, the majority of the educated youths have already achieved the work-point level of the local commune members.

The small group which joined the brigade is helped to develop collective supplementary production. Every production brigade has selected an old woman from among the poor peasants to act as consultant on living to the small groups which joined the brigade, who teaches them to raise pigs, feed chickens, plant vegetables, learn scientific home management, and regulate their lives. Every small group which joined the brigade has its vegetable plot, has raised chickens and ducks, fed pigs, and has sold food to the state in addition to that which they raised for their own use. At present, the majority of the educated youths can make a grain-use plan, save grain, and practice detailed planning and close reckoning. The educated youths who joined the

teams of the entire brigade have now all basically achieved
self-sufficiency in living.

3) Organize the Educated Youths to Develop Cultural and
Physical Activities. In accordance with the directive of Chairman Mao that "we must have a concern for the youth's study and
entertainment, physical training and rest, as well as for their
work," the brigade Party branch has emphasized organizing the
development of amateur cultural, entertainment, and physical
activities. The brigade set up an educated youth amateur culture and entertainment propaganda team and a library, built a
basketball court and a ping pong table, bought badminton shuttle-
cocks, and developed many different types of entertainment and
physical activities with the educated youths. This then improved
the physical and mental health of the youths, and enlivened the
amateur cultural life of the entire brigade, giving it a lively and
energetic appearance.

An-hui jih-pao [Anhwei Daily] Correspondent, An-hui jih-pao Reporter

6

Full Enthusiasm, Careful Work

Record of the Ch'ien-ying Brigade Party Branch Which Is Doing a Good Job with Educated Youths in the Countryside*

Ch'ien-ying is a production brigade in Hopei Province, Feng-Jung hsien, Hsin-chuang-tzu Commune, that has only some eighty families in it. At present, thirty-six educated youths have come to the countryside from T'ang-shan Municipality to join the brigade, make a home, and construct new socialist villages with the poor and lower-middle peasants.

In speaking of the work of the Ch'ien-ying Brigade Party branch with educated youths in the countryside, whether we consider it from the point of view of the youths, the poor and lower-middle peasants, or the parents of the youths in the countryside, all are very satisfied.

The youths in the countryside say, "Ch'ien-ying is our home, and the poor and lower-middle peasants are thus our family."

------

*Ch'ien-ying ta-tui tang-pu tso-hao hsia-hsiang ho chih-shih ch'ing-nien kung-tso ti shih-chi. "Man-k'ung je-ch'ing, kuo-hsi kung-tso."

In the past eight years, they have spent every Spring Festival with the poor and lower-middle peasants of Ch'ien-ying. In 1972, every person participated in 300 days of labor on the average and achieved basic self-sufficiency.

The poor and lower-middle peasants, seeing the youths develop a more and more active role in the countryside, say in praise, "This generation of young people has matured; when they came they did not know anything, now they are in the center of things! Surely they play a great part in changing the appearance of our villages."

The parents of the youths in the countryside say, "Ch'ien-ying Party branch and the poor and lower-middle peasants are even more concerned about the children then we are. What is there to be uneasy about?"

The youths in the countryside are at peace, the poor and lower-middle peasants are glad, the parents rest easy. How was this situation achieved?

The young people, recalling the course of tempering and maturing since they arrived in the countryside a few years ago, say with deep feeling, "The Party branch and the poor and lower-middle peasants have spent who knows how much effort on us!"

Bravely Shoulder Heavy Responsibility

In the autumn of 1965, before the first group of educated youths sent to the countryside arrived in the villages, certain cadres and masses had doubts. Some were worried that increasing the number of people without increasing the land would decrease the income; some felt that it would be a nuisance: "Bringing a group of bubbly raw children, what use is that? We'd just be worried about them!"

Should one worry or not? Does one dare to lead the poor and lower-middle peasants in worrying? In those days, the brigade Party secretary Hsü Min-kuang thought these questions over and over again. She restudied the glorious work of Chairman Mao "The Direction of the Youth Movement." She recalled her

own history of struggle in the past four years since she returned
in 1961 from T'ang-shan girl's high school to the countryside,
and came to a deep understanding that for youth to go up to the
mountains and down to the countryside to unite with workers
and peasants is important for carrying out the revolutionary
line of Chairman Mao and cultivating proletarian revolutionary
successors, and is necessary for the construction of new
socialist villages. Reliance on the poor and lower-middle
peasants and cultivating and educating the youths are questions
of attitude toward Chairman Mao and toward the revolutionary
work of the Party. The Party has given these educated youths
to us; it is only right that we worry about them. When I returned
to the countryside, was it not the Party organization and the
poor and lower-middle peasants who brought me to maturity by
cultivating and educating me bit by bit? She decided to shoulder
this extra revolutionary responsibility, not spare any effort,
and conscientiously do good work with educated youths in the
countryside.

Hsü Min-kuang invited the main cadres of the village to her
own home, and talked deep into the night for several nights.
By depending on the thought of Mao Tse-tung and by using the
progressive examples of Hsing Yen-tzu and Hou Ch'üan for
uniting with the poor and lower-middle peasants, she achieved
agreement in everyone's thinking. The comrades all expressed
the opinion, "Whatever Chairman Mao says, that we will do!
No matter how many educated youths come, we must cultivate
them well and educate them well, so that they may become the
cultured new peasants with socialist consciousness." After
unification of understanding was reached among the cadres,
repeated propaganda was carried out among the masses in
order to do a good job with educated youths and to put down a
good ideological foundation.

On August 17, 1965, the cadres and poor and lower-middle
peasants of Ch'ien-ying, beating drums and walking in procession
as though they were in a wedding ceremony, went up the highway
two li outside the village to welcome the educated youths who
were coming to join the brigade. They vacated the best house

for them and cleaned it, to let the young people live there; they made a dining table, small stools, and bellows for the young people; they also prepared a meal to welcome them.

After the educated youths joined the village, the Party branch appointed deputy secretary Wang Chang-ho to take special responsibility for working with educated youths; formed a leading group made up of representatives from the Party branch, the poor and lower-middle peasants, and the educated youths; selected enthusiastic poor and lower-middle peasants to take on the responsibility of being their tutors in politics, their teachers in production, and their consultants in living; and began to motivate the production brigade cadres and the Youth League and the Women's Association to be concerned about the educated youths.

The work of educating the educated youths was thus vigorously begun. But it was not long before some more questions of ideology came up.

One day, a production brigade leader reported to Hsü Min-kuang the circumstances of a youth in the countryside who was at loggerheads with him; he angrily said, "This blunt axe of mine cannot split this wart of an apricot tree; this burden I cannot carry!" Min-kuang studied with him Chairman Mao's directive on educated youth going up to the mountains and down to the countryside, and patiently talked with him, stimulating his sense of revolutionary responsibility. The old brigade leader was moved, and he said, "Ah! what I hate is that iron cannot become steel!" Hsü Min-kuang followed with, "Right, the trouble begins with this word 'hate.' Steel cannot be 'hated' into being, a hundred temperings are needed to make steel. We must use our deep proletarian feeling to work patiently, lead enthusiastically, and temper these young people into pieces of pure steel." The old brigade leader, hearing this, felt his heart grow warm and resolutely said that he would definitely not let down the expectations of Chairman Mao and the Party, and would educate the educated youths well and fully develop their usefulness.

Fiercely Struggle

The Ch'ien-ying Party branch, keeping in mind Chairman

Mao's directive that "we must never forget class struggle,"
has resolutely made foremost the task of changing the world
view of the educated youths and strengthening their concept of
class struggle in its work of cultivating and educating the educated youths.

On the second day after the educated youths arrived at the
village, the Party branch took them to nearby Che-chou Mountain, where the deputy secretary Wang Chang-ho introduced to
them the history of the class struggle in the village.

That autumn, when there was vigorous cultivation of the land,
the educated youths, encouraged by the revolutionary spirit of
fighting heaven and earth of the poor and lower-middle peasants,
did not fear the battle, and all fought to be among those doing
the work. Hsiao Sun of the No. 3 Production Team, his two
hands covered with bloody blisters, was urged to take a
rest, but he persisted in carrying on. The poor and lower-
middle peasants, seeing such revolutionary enthusiasm and
resolution in the young people, were glad in their hearts. However, not long after, a few of the more lively young people such
as Hsiao Sun became morose, quiet, and unenthusiastic in their
labor; when meetings were held for study, they were unwilling
to participate.

What was the cause of this? The cadres, poor and lower-
middle peasants, and some of the youths sent to the countryside
reported these circumstances to the Party branch.

It turned out that there was an old woman with a history of
being a counterrevolutionary who frequently made her way to
where Hsiao Sun and others lived, bringing them a few dishes,
a few sauces, and slyly saying, "Your life here is really so
bitter! If you were in town, living with your father and mother,
eating good rice and good dishes, then you would not be as you
are now!" Gust after gust of false wind and rain tore at the
thinking of Hsiao Sun and others, causing them to be confused.
That rascal even enticed Hsiao Sun and others to her home to
play and sing music, saying that they were going to set up a
"small club" and compete with the brigade's club.

The brigade Party branch analyzed and investigated these

circumstances and realized that this was a serious battle in the struggle between the bourgeoisie and the proletariat over the young people.

One night, when the youths held a meeting on livelihood, the Party branch led them to study conscientiously Chairman Mao's discussion of class struggle, and advanced a step in the revealing that person's reactionary history. Hsiao Sun and others were greatly surprised; when the meeting was over, it was already late at night, but they went to seek out Hsü Min-kuang at her home and said, "This giving of dishes and of sauces was really giving poison, pulling us downriver!" Hsü Min-kuang encouraged them to learn a lesson from this, to raise their understanding of class struggle, and to walk with the poor and lower-middle peasants. Since that time, these young people have again become active.

The educated youth Hsiao Ma was enthusiastic at the beginning of the Cultural Revolution. Not long after, a class enemy in the village discovered his weaknesses of being disorganized in his actions and of loving to eat well and drink well, and so stretched out a black hand to entice him, causing Hsiao Ma to commit a serious error.

After the brigade revolutionary committee was set up, some comrades suggested criticism of Hsiao Ma,; Hsiao Ma's father also wrote to ask the revolutionary committee and the poor and lower-middle peasants of Ch'ien-ying Brigade to sternly criticize Hsiao Ma. Hsü Min-kuang and other comrades felt that there should be a strict distinction between two types of contradictions, that Hsiao Ma is a class brother who was taken advantage of by enemies, and that he should be helped and united with. Hsü Min-kuang also introduced to the comrades the direction of the class enemy. She said, "In the past, class enemies used Hsiao Ma to attack us; now class enemies also dream of our criticizing and struggling down Hsiao Ma, so that they can get the better of us from two directions. We must not fall into the deceitful trap of the enemy."

Helping Hsiao Ma was truly a difficult and formidable task. Hsü Min-kuang twice sought out Hsiao Ma to talk, without success either time. She repeatedly thought over the structure of Hsiao Ma's thinking, and again went to his dwelling, and using bitterness to draw out bitterness, she aroused Hsiao Ma's class consciousness and said to him, "You are walking upon a stretch of curved road in the movement; the problem begins with you, the responsibility lies with us. We have not helped you enough, and thus let down Chairman Mao and your parents." As Hsiao Ma listened, he could no longer sit still. "Min-kuang, older sister, please don't go on. It is all because my consciousness is low that I was taken in by the enemy and took the wrong path. It is I who let down the Party, let down Chairman Mao, and turned my back on the poor and lower-middle peasants." That day Hsü Min-kuang and Hsiao Ma talked thoroughly for a long, long time, together recollecting past bitterness and thinking about present sweetness. She helped him analyze the circumstances of the class struggle in Ch'ien-ying. Once awakened to the truth, Hsiao Ma was full of hatred and exposed a great many crimes of class enemies. After that, Hsiao Ma always comported himself well and improved very quickly.

The two fierce class struggles deeply educated the Party branch of Ch'ien-ying Brigade and even more deeply taught the educated youths in the countryside that class struggle is truly a principal concern of youth. Since then, the Party branch has frequently invited old poor peasants who had known deep hatred and resentment to talk with the educated youths, recalling past bitterness and present sweetness; it has organized the educated youths to carry out social investigations, to write a history of the village and of families, and to open up an exhibit hall on class education. They were tempered in the front line of real class struggle which helped them ceaselessly raise their consciousness of class struggle and line struggle.

Correctly Lead

Directing the students not to forget to read books and study while engaged in production and to raise their consciousness of line struggle is an important theme that the Ch'ien-ying

Brigade Party branch frequently emphasizes. At one point, the educated youths in the countryside felt that productive labor was so time consuming and tiring that there was no time to read and study; with the poor and lower-middle peasants to lead the way, it did not matter whether one read. In response to this situation, the Party branch and the educated youths studied together relevant discussions of Chairman Mao, raised their study consciousness and emphasized the need to unite with and be reeducated by the poor and lower-middle peasants and to earnestly read and study. It frequently organized the youths to connect the reality of the Three Great Revolutionary Movements with the earnest study of the books of Marx and Lenin and the books of Chairman Mao, in order to reconstruct their world view.

The educated youths sent to the countryside, under the warm concern of the Party branch and the poor and lower-middle peasants, raised their ideological consciousness, took a firm hold on the basic skills of production, and in order to change the backward production conditions of Ch'ien-ying Brigade as quickly as possible, requested the development of scientific experimentation in agriculture. The Party branch warmly encouraged and supported the young people's revolutionary activism; the brigade allotted twenty mou of good land for experimental fields, and an old poor peasant, Wang Hua-kuan, vacated two rooms for them to use as laboratories. The poor and lower-middle peasants proudly said, "With this bunch of youngsters to do experiments, we needn't worry about being able to take off the hat of low production."

When scientific experimentation began, the young people borrowed from their alma mater microscopes and a soil analysis kit, found a lot of books on scientific technique, and shut themselves in the laboratory the whole day studying. They did not pay attention to what the poor and lower-middle peasants had to say; they looked down on the old peasants' experiments; today they thought of doing this, the next day they thought of doing that; right away they set up twenty-six items for research, always thinking of producing something new with which to startle people. They fantasized about interbreeding the cotton shoot with the paulownia to produce a "cotton tree," so that without yearly planting they could get yearly harvests of cotton; they also fantasized grafting "baimaya" corn to glutinous corn to create "Ch'ien-ying No. 1," "young people's speciality," and other types of new products.

They experimented one by one with these projects, and one by one with a brave beginning and weak ending [lit. tiger's head, snake's tail] they stopped work on them. Some of the experiments were failures; some had no practical use even though there seemed to be some result to show for it. People began to say, "These 'foreign scholars' have only been farming from books; for our village to change its profile of low production, we cannot look to them." The young people struggled on alone for the greater part of the year, but their labor showed no results and their hearts became heavy.

This situation aroused the attention of the Party branch, and at the opportune moment it held a scientific experimentation meeting and organized the young people to study Chairman Mao's teaching that "if the educated youths do not mutually unite with the workers, peasants, and masses of people, they will not accomplish a single thing." While affirming their revolutionary fervor, the Party branch also earnestly pointed out to them their mistaken tendency of having "scientific experimentation and production practicality two different layers of skin, and separating the scientific technique group from the cadres and masses"; and it criticized their idea of giving a name to their project before they had any results, and of trying to astound people. Thus they corrected the direction in which they were moving. Then they set up a scientific experimentation three-in-one small group made up of cadres, poor and lower-middle peasants, and educated youths, under the responsibility of the Party branch deputy secretary Wang Chieh-lun.

The line was straight; the direction was clear. After this the scientific experimentation group started from the reality of the agricultural production of Ch'ien-ying, open-mindedly sought advice from the poor and lower-middle peasants, and took as their chief goals the improvement of cultivation systems, the

selection and cultivation of good strains, the eradication of pests
and diseases, the production and use of microbes and such subjects, and they worked hard to make them reality. The youth
Ho Chen-fang frequently went about in the wind and rain, going
from one observation point to another, earnestly recording the
condition of insects. Once, for three nights in a row, carrying
a storm lantern, he crouched on the ground meticulously observ-
ing the circumstances of the growth and life of insects. After
much hard work, a method was eventually found to prevent and
cure the effects of six types of harmful insects and yet was
suitable to local conditions. With good results it controlled
destruction done by the insects. The masses enthusiastically
called him "King of the Insects." The scientific experimentation
group, using only twenty yuan [about $10.00], set up a small
lab for microbes, and with only rough working conditions, the
young people successfully developed the "920" biological element [sheng-wu chi-su (?)] and the "5406" fungus fertilizer.
Moreover, they produced these on a large scale. In addition, they
experimented with developing earth mildew elements used in farming and phospherous bacteria fertilizer. They also brought in and
selected for cultivation sixty-one types of good strains of grain,
cotton, and oil crops, and promoted on a large scale the planting
of eight superior strains that were suited to local conditions.
Because of the practicality and the promotion of the results of
these scientific experiments, they were the first step in changing
the low production profile of Ch'ien-ying. In the past, the
grain production was two or three hundred chin per mou, but
since 1967, year after year production has crossed the "Yellow
River," cotton production was increased from 40 chin of raw
cotton balls per mou to 115 chin; peanuts production was increased from 100 chin per mou to more than 300 chin.

Patiently Educate

It is a long-term process for the educated youths to walk upon
the road of mutually uniting with the poor and lower-middle
peasants. To educate them to set down roots in the villages

requires a great deal of difficult and detailed ideological work. The poor and lower-middle peasants of Ch'ien-ying Brigade put it well: "Educating the educated youths is like growing cotton; enough water and plenty of fertilizer and they will grow large. If you want to have fruit from cotton plants you have to prune vigorously."

The Party branch of Ch'ien-ying Brigade was exactly like this. It did not depend on a gust of wind, but used ideological work that had been thought out in detail. Ideological waves were easy to produce, especially when the educated youths met with some difficulty, experienced some setbacks, or when the time came for factory work applications, student applications, or returning from visiting their families. The Party branch always opportunely and patiently did a good job of education in setting down roots.

Once, the brigade leader Li Feng-ling, after assigning the heavy work, assigned the three relatively weak female educated youths who were left to the light job of picking cotton. These three young girls picked for a long time in the cotton fields, and still had not covered the bottom of the basket; they looked at the long furrows and began to fear difficulties. "How long do we have to do this work before we see the end of it!" One youth's words had scarcely been spoken when another continued, "Some classmates have entered the factories in the cities, while all day long we deal with this wretched land, what's the point!" The three of them, following with comments one upon the other, became more confused as they talked. The Party branch, after it understood this situation, organized them to learn the relevant directives of Chairman Mao, helped them to accurately understand ideals and the future. The poor peasant Wang Hsi-chen, with earnest words and a kind heart, said to them, "It isn't that the field is large; it's that your thinking is small!" After this, the three girls improved very quickly; they all joined the Youth League; one of them even joined the Party and became the brigade Youth League branch deputy secretary and a member of the hsien-wide Youth League committee.

Last summer, there were a few educated youths who felt that

having been working in the countryside for some six or seven
years, their thinking and their labor had shown some results,
and they hoped for an opportunity to leave the village to go to
school. The Party branch, seeing the appearance of such thinking in these educated youths in the countryside, used three days'
time to organize the young people to study the directives of
Chairman Mao and to study the essay "Follow the Party's
Arrangements in Everything" by comrade Lu Yü-lan and opened
a discussion on the topic, "correct attitudes toward ideals and
the future." In this meeting the Party branch secretary Hsü
Min-kuang spoke of what she had learned from her own experience in setting down roots in the village to carry out revolution.
The educated youths, after study and discussion, raised their
consciousness; they said, to realize communism, to realize the
thorough liberation of all of mankind is the highest form of
ideals; to devote one's life to struggle for the revolution is the
best future. To advance on the golden road of mutually uniting
with the workers and peasants as indicated by Chairman Mao
is glory without end and well-being without limit.

After the educated youths had truly understood the deep and
far-reaching meaning of setting down roots in the villages, they
grew to love even more warmly the poor and lower-middle peasants and the villages. They say that the villages are a vast
universe, that there is knowledge there that can be learned without end, that there is an unending mission there. When Ch'ien-
ying received from above the applications for work and for
study, everyone deferred to each other; no one wanted to leave
this place. In the people's movement to learn from Tachai in
agriculture, they all contributed their share, carrying heavy
burdens, fighting the first battle, always saying, "Even if sweat
falls from every pore, we must 'force ourselves across the
Yangtze.'" The poor and lower-middle peasants praise them
as "good commune members in the style of Tachai," and happily
say, "The coming of the educated youths to the countryside is
truly a case of good iron tempered into steel."

Among the educated youths sent to the countryside, some are
"sons and daughters who can be educated well." Toward these

young people, the brigade Party branch always takes the initiative in getting to know them better and propagates among them matters that are emphasized by the Party. However, these matters are not discussed alone; what is emphasized is the political manifestation of proletarian policy, so that they will understand clearly that their birth cannot be chosen, but that the revolutionary road can be chosen. One needs only to take the stand of the proletariat in order to have a bright future. When one educated youth first came to the countryside his thought bore the heavy burden of his family background; frequently in meeting a problem he walked around it, and in study discussions he seldom spoke. The comrades of the Party branch realized what he was thinking and many times sought him out to talk and warmly help him, so that he developed a revolutionary spirit. In the area of scientific experimentation, he became very useful and attended with glory the provincial, regional, and hsien meetings of the representatives of educated youths.

At present, of the entire brigade's thirty-six educated youths who have come to the countryside, eight have become cadres in the brigades, the production teams, the militia companies, and the Communist Youth League; many have become technicians, veterinarians, electricians, carpenters, and teachers in popularly managed schools. They are developing greater and greater usefulness in the villages.

Show Warm Concern

The Ch'ien-ying Brigade Party branch followed the directive of Chairman Mao that "we should deeply concern ourselves with the question of the livelihood of the masses" and frequently placed livelihood problems of educated youths on the agenda to be resolved through discussion.

In the winter of 1965, the Party branch investigated the problem of setting up housing for the young people in the countryside. Some comrades said, "How much one eats depends on how much food there is; to make clothing one has to measure the person;

let's see how much money is set aside from above, and then we can build that many houses. If it's not enough, then they can crowd a little." Once this suggestion was made, the meeting became very lively and enthusiastic discussion began. What principle should really be followed — should we investigate this problem simply from the point of view of economics, or should we emphasize the political aspect? Should problems be dealt with as they come up, or should there be long-term considerations? Hsü Min-kuang said, "We must begin by thinking that the educated youths are setting down roots in the village for the long term; we should build as many houses as are needed. If conditions are right for raising a little money we should do it." After discussion, a consensus was reached and it was decided to build eleven houses.

After two months of careful work, a row of brand new one-story brick houses was built, and the young people happily moved into the spacious new quarters.

In 1970 the second group of educated youths arrived in the village. Some comrades said, "Last time each production brigade raised some money for building houses. This time it's not necessary to build houses again. Let's give the money to the production team to develop agricultural production." The Party branch held that the state had set aside this amount of money with which to build housing for the educated youths and special funds must be used for their designated purpose. In addition, in a few years the young people will be older and ought to be marrying; how can they manage if we do not first prepare housing for them to use after marriage? The Party branch, after investigation, again built ten new one-story brick houses for them.

In July 1966, after the young people had moved into the new housing, they immediately merged the three dining halls and kitchens that had existed in the production team into one collective dining hall. Under the tutelage and help of the Party branch and the poor and lower-middle peasants, the educated youths, who originally did not understand how to plan the use of grain and how to economically use grain, gradually learned how to calculate everything closely, to economize grain and to use fuel sparingly. The comrades show mutual concern for each other and unite in friendship. If some comrades have to take a trip on some task, the comrades responsible for food get up in the middle of the night to prepare food for them to take along; if some comrades become sick, the kitchen specially prepares invalid meals for them; for the New Year and for festivals, the comrades who are away are brought back to eat dinner with the group; even for comrades who are returning to their families, they specially prepare a meal. In these eight years, the youth's collective dining hall is managed better and better.

Time passes and age increases. The brigade Party branch, while educating the educated youths to marry late is also appropriately concerned about the question of marriage for those young people of a greater age. At present, some of the women educated youths have married young men from this village, and some of the young educated men and women have married each other. After the young people are married, the Party branch educates and helps them to arrange properly their household affairs and to participate actively in political study and in every type of activity. In the earthshaking struggle of Ch'ien-ying they still continue to play active roles.

In these eight years, the educated youths and the poor and lower-middle peasants of Ch'ien-ying Brigade have developed a deep class feeling for each other. The poor and lower-middle peasants warmly love the educated youths, and the educated youths also warmly love the poor and lower-middle peasants. The poor and lower-middle peasants say that the Party and Chairman Mao have handed over these children to us, we must be even more concerned for them than for our own children. Once, when a youth caught a heavy cold, six families of poor and lower-middle peasants, without consulting with each other, all sent over chicken eggs, goat's milk, hot noodle soup, etc. One youth came down with rheumatic arthritis, and the old brigade leader Hsü Kuo-kuang brought him to his own house, where the youth lived for more than a year on the warm k'ang.

Because of the warm concern of the poor and lower-middle

peasants, the advanced collective of educated youths who have come to live in Ch'ien-ying Brigade, like so many clusters of bright flowers, have grown strongly under the sunlight of the thought of Mao Tse-tung. One can see that these young people, who a few years ago were still children, jumping about, unable to tell grass from crops, have actually grown into an indispensable force in every aspect of work at Ch'ien-ying Brigade. The brigade Party branch and the poor and lower-middle peasants, looking on the past, feel their hearts fill with exhilaration; looking into the future, they feel their confidence increase manyfold. They are determined to make even greater efforts to educate these educated youths even better to fully develop their active role in the vast universe, and to let their youth emit even greater radiance.

Kuang-ming jih-pao correspondent,
Kuang-ming jih-pao reporter

7

How We Cultivated the Growth of Hou Chün
under the Leadership of the Party

The Poor and Lower-Middle Peasants
of Tu-chia-ch'iao Brigade, Pao-ti Hsien*

It has already been a full ten years since Comrade Hou Chün
came from Peking to join our Tu-chia-ch'iao Brigade and make
a home. In these ten years, under the education of the Party,
Hou Chün grew quickly and changed from an ordinary middle
school student into the new type of peasant; she was selected by
us poor and lower-middle peasants to enter the brigade leadership ranks and to become our good leader. This is entirely the
result of being nurtured by the thought of Mao Tse-tung and is
a victory of the revolutionary line of Chairman Mao. In the
process of her growth, especially at pivotal times of struggle
between two lines, the Party central leadership comrades and
Party organizations on every level have shown very warm

_____

*Pao-ti hsien Tu-chia-ch'iao ta-tui p'in-hsia-chung-nung,
"Wo-men shih tsen-yang tsai tang ti ling-tao hsia p'ei-yang
Hou Chün ch'eng-chang ti."

concern and provided education at the right times. From this process we poor and lower-middle peasants have been educated and stimulated, and even more deeply understand the importance of doing a good job of reeducation.

In the following pages we describe how we followed the teachings of Chairman Mao, and under the direct leadership of the Party branch, cultivated the growth of Hou Chün.

Special Emphasis Must Be Placed on Changing the Ideals of Youth into the Reality of Revolution

In 1962 Hou Chün came from Peking to make a home in our Tu-chia-ch'iao Brigade. At that time, it was still an unusual thing for a student from the city to come to the village. Some indecisive types were against it. They said, "The students come to the villages, but after a few days novelty wears off and they leave. Why not have her leave right away." Was this true? We asked Hou Chün, "Why did you come to Tu-chia-ch'iao?" She said, "To work at agriculture and to work at food production in response to the great call of the Party and of Chairman Mao and to build new socialist villages!" We were very happy to hear Hou Chün say this. We then said, "Our Tu-chia-ch'iao is a poor place. Are you afraid of hardship coming here?" She then said, "I am not afraid! The more trying the environment, the better one is tempered." On hearing this, who would not be touched to the heart and welcome a young person with such determination?

Hou Chün is a good young shoot; she has the determination to stay in the village and carry out a lifetime of revolution, and she has the long-term ideal of constructing new socialist villages. When she first arrived in the villages to work, it happened to be the hottest season, the time for hoeing the late corn. Above, the sun beat on the head; below, the earth gave off heat; without even working, one's whole body would be soaked with sweat. When she first used a hoe, if she didn't lift it high up and let it fall so that it clanged and clattered, she thrust it low into the ground and couldn't move it; she used a lot of energy, a lot of sweat, and what she hoed was uneven, with footprints all over it, often packing down what had just been hoed. Hou Chün was angry and felt stupid. An old poor peasant, Chang Fu-te, persuaded her not to be impatient: "Hoeing is also like learning to write; the more you practice, the better you get." While he talked, he patiently showed Hou Chün the skills of hoeing. In this way, Hou Chün studied whatever she was doing. She studied what she did and we taught her what she wanted to learn. Once, under the light of the moon, Hou Chün was practicing hoeing in the fields. A poor peasant, Chang Ch'ing-t'ien, saw her and went over to teach her. Done once, something is still new; done twice, something becomes familiar. Slowly, Hou Chün learned something of farming skills.

Although Hou Chün was full of determination when she first arrived in the village, she had some doubts after some time had passed. Hou Chün is a person who likes to talk and sing. But there was a spell when she did not talk or sing in the rest period after work. What was the real cause of this? In casual conversations, we discovered her state of mind. She felt that life in the villages was all work, busy and hectic, but nothing great and inspiring could be done.

When Hou Chün came to the countryside, her thinking was far-reaching and her will strong, how was it that she was now vacillating? We poor and lower-middle peasants gathered together many times to mull over this problem. Some said, "People who study change their minds really fast. Wind today, rain tomorrow. Their moods aren't stable." Some said, "Young people are overly ambitious. Whatever they do, it's only with three minutes of enthusiasm." All comments referred to the instability of young people.

Why is it that an educated youth like Hou Chün who was determined to carry out revolution in the village still vacillated? We analyzed her thinking and actions before and after she came to the village, and felt that this was the problem: the educated youths who were born and grew up in the time of Mao Tse-tung all love the Party, all love Chairman Mao, and all love socialism. They all want to achieve something in the construction of socialism. This is their far-reaching ideal. This kind of ideal is of course good; however, if ideals are not united with reality, they become daydreams, and if daydreams are not realized, vacillation results and nothing is done. In reality, a gap still exists between the ideals of the young people and reality. Thus we emphasized education in ideals and in the future, letting the young people understand that building a great communist edifice depends on piling up each brick and each tile, depends on our exertions drop by drop. Our ordinary labor hoe and sickle have a very close connection with socialist revolution and socialist construction and a very close mutual connection with supporting world revolution.

One day we selected and studied with Hou Chün a saying of Chairman Mao: "Today's hard work is directed toward the great goal of the future; to lose this great goal is no longer to be a Communist Party member. Similarly to slacken in today's hard work is no longer to be a Communist Party member." Hou Chün was most receptive to Chairman Mao's words, and after studying them, her thinking slowly straightened out. She said, "The far-reaching ideals of revolutionary youth must keep the overall situation in mind and keep in sight the Chinese revolution and the world revolution; we must stick to our work and start by making more contributions to the revolution. In the past, I lacked the spirit of firmly and bitterly struggling to realize the far-reaching ideal of liberation of all of mankind!" After this episode, we better understood our responsibilities, the first of which was to educate the educated youths to understand that to change ideals into reality requires hard struggle and hard labor. Communism does not fall out of the sky; it doesn't come out as we sit waiting on the k'ang, but requires our persistent hard work. It must also be clearly understood that those people who are overly ambitious, who think of leaving, will never accomplish any great "inspiring" deed.

We Must Push the Young People into the Front Line of the Three Great Revolutionary Movements to Be Tempered

After her understanding of ideals and realism was raised,

Hou Chün's enthusiasm for labor was even higher, and her willingness to endure hardship was even greater. During the wheat harvest of 1963, Hou Chün was cutting wheat for the first time. She didn't know how to do it, and wasn't very enthusiastic about it. But Hou Chün was tempering herself and worked hard at harvesting the wheat. Before long, her hands developed seven or eight blood blisters. When we saw that her hands were being rubbed badly, we were grieved and wouldn't let her go on, no matter what. But Hou Chün said, "If I don't learn this year, next year I still wouldn't know how to do it!" She gritted her teeth and continued to pull the wheat. With this kind of energetic involvement, working seemed to become part of her being. After a few month's Hou Chün became much stronger, and her farming skills improved. At that time, someone said, "Hou Chün's heart is completely in her labor; now she has truly set down roots in the village."

This statement awakened us to the question, Is simply laboring hard the same as setting down roots? We poor and lower-middle peasants again gathered together to discuss this matter. The educated youths do not come to the countryside only to increase the labor force; they come so that they may develop an even greater role in the vast universe of the villages! How could it be enough only to ask Hou Chün to bury herself in production? Discussing this, everyone came to understand that in cultivating Hou Chün we could not depend only on labor; we had to place her in the front lines of the Three Great Revolutionary Movements to be tempered.

In the winter of 1963, our village initiated a rousing socialist education movement. We specifically focused on the condition of Hou Chün's thought and pushed her to the front lines of the class struggle, so that she could receive class education in the fiery heat of the class struggle and raise her ideological consciousness. In that socialist education movement, Hou Chün heard with her own ears the old poor peasants accuse the landlord class, and personally participated in real class struggle, increasing her understanding that in the old society: one rich family, ten thousand poor; one village, two worlds. She more deeply understood Chairman Mao's teaching: "In the historical period of socialism, there still remain classes, class contradictions, and class struggle; there still remains the struggle between the two roads of socialism and capitalism; there still remains the danger of the restoration of capitalism." Confronted by the reality of class struggle, Hou Chün compared the past to the present and increased her love for the Party, for Chairman Mao, and for socialism. She said, "I received more from one experience of real class education than I had in ten years of classroom education. I resolve to unceasingly raise my consciousness of class struggle and line struggle, and all my life walk the road of uniting with the workers and peasants."

We did not feel self-satisfied about Hou Chün's progress, however. The more quickly she grew, the more we felt the increased difficulties of the responsibilities of reeducation. How could she achieve even greater progress? How could we create conditions for her growth?

In the beginning of 1965, we organized a small scientific experimentation group around Hou Chün in order to develop to the utmost the special qualities of youth. Hou Chün and the poor and lower-middle peasants set up experiments in sand dune control and soil management in the sandy wilds of Nan-wa, which in past years had never produced more than 100 chin of grain per mou. We dug ditches and made canals, built up land and soaked the dunes, and in one spring we created 250 mou of arable land in strips and terraces. This autumn we gathered an unprecedented good harvest of more than 500 chin of corn per mou. Besides this, we helped Hou Chün organize educated youths in the countryside to go to the commune masses to read newspapers, tell revolutionary stories, and teach revolutionary songs, taking over the cultural battleground of the villages. When they return at noon, they write bulletins on the blackboard, broadcast local affairs, and propagate the directives of the Party. In the evenings, they go to evening classes to study the works of Chairman Mao with the commune masses.

We have resolutely set our sights on cultivating successors

to the proletarian revolutionary cause and have pushed Hou
Chün onto the front lines of the Three Great Revolutionary
Movements so that she may experience winds and rains, see
the world, and increase in ability and mature quickly through
struggle. Practice has proved that this is an important condition for reeducating educated youths. It correctly deals with
the dialectical relationship between education and application,
and it can fully supply the content for reeducation and raise the
level of reeducation work.

Use the Five Conditions and Strict Demands of Chairman Mao for Cultivating Successors to the Proletarian Revolutionary Cause

Following the tempering and testing of the Proletarian Cultural Revolution, Hou Chün even more resolutely advanced
along the great revolutionary road of mutually uniting with the
workers and peasants. She was sequentially selected to be a
committee member of the local committee and hsien committee,
the secretary of the brigade Party branch, and the chairman of
the revolutionary committee.

At this point, somebody again said, "This time everything is
set. Hou Chün is now a cadre, she has the authority to go on,
reeducation has reached its end, our educational responsibilities
are finally finished." Are we poor and lower-middle peasants
to remain as Hou Chün's teachers or are we not? Hou Chün
said, "My position has changed, but being reeducated cannot
change. I am always the little student of the poor and lower-
middle peasants." As events proved, Hou Chün spoke correctly. After she became a cadre, she made severe demands
on herself in every way; her enthusiasm was high and her willingness to work great. Last year, at the beginning of spring,
the ground was still frozen and the north wind was still bone
chilling. In order to continue constructing fields of high quality,
we masses of poor and lower-middle peasants again began the
basic construction of new farmlands. Constructing farmlands
on a large scale requires filling in the swamps by moving great

quantities of earth. At the time not only was the ground frozen
like stone, but also the distance for transporting the earth was
too far, and there was insufficient transportation equipment.
Seeing this situation, some people wanted to hold out their hands
and ask the state for an earth-moving machine. At this time,
Hou Chün, thinking of getting the fields in order as quickly as
possible, also felt that there ought to be an earth-moving machine. The old branch secretary and old poor peasant Tsao
Hsüeh-yen found Hou Chün and said, "We can't depend on the
state in building socialism; we can't depend on outside help;
we must depend on our own revolutionary will, depend on the
revolutionary spirit of self-reliance and bitter struggle!" On
hearing this, Hou Chün was greatly educated and took the lead by
buying a handcart. Following her lead, the entire brigade suddenly acquired more than fifty handcarts and greatly increased
the progress of the work, and in less than a month's time,
moved more than 10,000 sections of earth, constructed 75
mou of fields and dug an irrigating canal. In the same year
in which this piece of land was transformed, it produced, on the
average, almost 400 chin per mou in the summer harvest
season.

Not only do we make strict demands of Hou Chün, we also
support her in working boldly and developing a greater role.
Last winter we collected and stored fertilizer. In the morning
the work was voluntary, and work points were not given. Hou
Chün felt that it did not fulfill the principle of "reward for
work done" and suggested some ways of improving this. We
poor and lower-middle peasants said that she was right and
resolutely supported her; thus, she and the Party branch together very quickly passed down the relevant policies.

In the course of practice, we also learned that in order to
advance unceasingly the work of reeducation, we poor and lower-
middle peasants must ourselves unceasingly reconstruct our
thinking. "To be a good teacher, one must first be a good student." When the level of thinking is raised, then the work of
reeducation is done better and better. Once Hou Chün and
the Party branch member, old poor peasant Chang Fu-t'ung,

returned together from a commune meeting when it was almost
time to quit work. Hou Chün wanted to go home quickly to prepare dinner, for in the evening she still have to tell about the
spirit of the meeting. Chang Fu-t'ung also wanted to go home,
but he turned over the thought that he carried the heavy responsibility of educating the youth and ought to be a good model to
the youth in every way. Thus he quickly went into the fields to
join in the labor. Chung Fu-t'ung's action was an unvoiced criticism of Hou Chün and at the same time an example to her:
after becoming a cadre, it is even more important to participate in collective productive labor and to never become separated from the masses.

After this incident, Hou Chün was very conscious of joining
in the collective productive labor. Once the commune was holding a meeting and notified her that the meeting would start at
2:30 promptly. But after lunch she still went with the commune
members to dig ditches. We asked her, "Aren't you going to
the commune meeting?" Hou Chün laughed and said, "It is
still more than an hour away; I won't be late if I work for a
bit." And it was thus that after working for a while she arrived
at the meeting on time perspiring all over from the work.

On seeing Hou Chün make such strict demands on herself,
all of us increased our concern for her and warmly helped her.
Sometimes when a problem appeared, we did not wait for her to
come and seek advice, but voluntarily went over to help; for
example, the old poor peasants Kuan Yu-ch'eng and Chang Fu-te
are both good teachers who went to offer help.

This is the way we treated Hou Chün, and it is the same for
other educated youths in the countryside. In our Tu-chia-ch'iao
there are still six educated youths who have been sent to the
countryside. After cultivation and education, some of them have
become cadres, some have become teachers, some have become
propaganda workers, agricultural technicians, and health
workers. All have become very useful in the villages.

It has been more than four years since Chairman Mao de-
livered his great directive that "educated youths must go to
the villages and receive reeducation from the poor and lower-

middle peasants. We must persuade the cadres and others in the cities to send their sons and daughters who have graduated from lower-middle school, upper-middle school, and universities to the countryside and make it a campaign. Comrades in villages everywhere should welcome their going." Studying this every day makes it seem even more relevant. Chairman Mao has given to us poor and lower-middle peasants the heavy responsibility of educating the educated youths; this shows the greatest trust in us. We must earnestly follow Chairman Mao's great teaching and warmly welcome the educated youths coming to the villages. We must look after them warmly, take full responsibility, teach patiently, and use these youths boldly. We must contribute our total strength in cultivating the successors to the proletarian revolutionary cause for our socialist country.

8

Consolidate and Develop the Great Achievements of Educated Youths Who Have Gone up to the Mountains and down to the Countryside

The Kuei-chou Neighborhood of Nanking East Road in Shanghai Municipality Coordinates with the Villages in Doing Good Reeducation Work*

Since 1968, more than 600 educated youths from the Kuei-chou Neighborhood of Nanking East Road, Whangpoo District, Shanghai, have responded to the call of our great leader Chairman Mao that "educated youths must go to the villages and receive reeducation from the poor and lower-middle peasants." They have gone to the villages in every part of the country and to the border regions to make revolution. After sending off these educated youths, some of the cadres of the neighborhood thought, "Our responsibilities are finished. We can relax." However,

---

*Shang-hai shih Nan-ching tung lu Kuei-chou li-nung p'ei-ho nung-ts'un kao-hao tsai-chiao-yü. "K'ung-ku ho fa-chan chih-shih ch'ing-nien shang-shan hsia-hsiang ti wei-ta ch'eng-kuo."

after some time passed, some of the young people in the villages met with difficulties and vacillated in their thinking; and some parents were anxious because their sons and daughters had gone far away. The neighborhood branch realized that if it did not immediately help the parents resolve this problem, it would not only affect their adherence to revolution and promotion of production but, more importantly, it would adversely affect the cultivation of successors to the proletarian revolution. It was at this time that a group of parents of educated youths voluntarily organized small groups to discuss together the problem of how to educate sons and daughters to set down roots in the villages. The Party branch immediately latched onto this newborn thing and set about mobilizing the masses, organizing the parents to study the series of directives of Chairman Mao concerning the movement of educated youths up to the mountains and down to the countryside in order to raise their consciousness of line struggle, so that they would actively coordinate with the resettlment area in doing a good job of reeducating the educated youths.

In order to strengthen its leadership in this work, this neighborhood in February 1971 set up a "leadership group to coordinate reeducation work with the villages." (Education Coordinating Group [P'ei-chiao-tsu], for short.) It was made up mainly of parents and included retired workers, spare-time propaganda team members, and neighborhood cadres, seventeen people in all. This group studied the experience of Ch'ing-huo residential area in Yangchow City and voluntarily coordinated with the villages to reeducate educated youths in the countryside; it became a main force in the neighborhood for promoting this work.

Clearly Distinguish the Line   Raise Consciousness

The "Education Coordinating Group" understood from practice that in order to do a good job of consolidating up to the mountains, down to the countryside work, so that young people will set down roots in the villages, it is necessary to raise the consciousness of parents concerning the struggle between two lines. In response to the concern of some parents that their children are too far from home, and to their great concern about living conditions and small concern for politics, and to the fact that their sons and daughters did not have adequate ideological preparation to remain in the villages and be peasants for a lifetime, the group members, from the start, placed ideological and political education at the forefront. In the past two years, they have maintained a system of scheduled study once a week and held many kinds of criticism meetings. They also set up five revolutionary criticism bulletin boards throughout the neighborhood and posted numerous articles, criticizing swindlers like Liu Shao-ch'i who disseminate reactionary, specious theories such as landlord and bourgeois "individualism," "the end of class struggle," "go to the countriside to acquire gold-plating," "study to become an official," "disguised reform through labor," and so on. Through these articles, the political awareness of the parents was raised.

Yü Huan-fang, the parent of an educated youth, was somewhat anxious when her child left for Heilungkiang. She was afraid he would meet a wild animal while on guard duty at night; she was afraid he would be bitten by a poisonous snake when sleeping outside at night. She sent letter after letter, telling him "not to run too far ahead." Apparently Yü Huan-fang still thought that this was the way "fathers and mothers love their children" and was "normal human affection." Following study and revolutionary criticism, she understood that love has a class nature, that different classes use different thoughts and feelings to influence their sons and daughters. She said, with deep understanding, "Although a letter is only a few sheets of paper, what you say actually reflects the struggle between two types of thinking, two lines. I have been affected by the poison of 'individualism' touted by swindlers like Liu Shao-ch'i and have affected my child's tempering and growth in the villages. This is not loving one's child but harming one's child." After this, when Yü Huan-fang learned that her child was working as a dynamite blaster on the site of a water reservoir, she

encouraged in him the revolutionary spirit of "first, not fearing
hardship, second not fearing death"; and to be like Chin Hsün-
hua who said that one should "work as hard as possible as long
as one is alive, and give one's life to Chairman Mao!" She
herself also resolved to learn from Chin Hsün-hua's mother
and to be a revolutionary mother.

Promote Progress	Masses Teach Each Other

After unceasing elevation of line struggle consciousness of
revolutionary parents, there emerged some progressive models
who "teach their sons and daughters to engage in agriculture."
The "Education Coordinating Group" put much effort into prop-
agating these models so that the masses could become enlight-
ened, teach themselves, and advance the revolutionary enthusiasm of the masses of parents for teaching their sons and
daughters to engage in agriculture.

Juan Ching-wen, a parent of educated youths, sent four children to the villages. The third child joined a brigade and settled down in Heilungkiang. The authorities approved his transfer to a factory. The child wrote a letter home, saying, I have
resolved to be with the masses of poor and lower-middle peasants, and change the appearance of the mountain valley where
they live in the spirit of the foolish old man who removed the
mountains. Juan Ching-wen felt that her child had revolutionary
determination and resolutely supported his wish. The "Education Coordinating Group" made the progressive case of Juan
Ching-wen widely known and invited her to discuss her understanding and knowledge in a parents meeting held in the neighborhood.

The force of example is without end. Wang Hsiu-chüan, a
parent of educated youths, was an orphan in the old society.
After liberation, she had a strong sense of having turned herself around. She loved Chairman Mao and the Communist Party
deeply. In recent years, she has responded to Chairman Mao's
call and sent three sons and daughters to the villages. However, when she saw that a neighbor's child had been selected

to leave the villages and to be transferred to a factory in the city, she thought of how other people's children can come back, live close to the family, and have better living conditions; thus she began to think that "going to the countryside was to get the worst of it." After being educated about the exemplary deeds of Juan Ching-wen and other comrades, she began to recollect the bitterness of her youth in the old society, and in turn this gave rise to proletarian feeling; she understood that she should not be selfish and have these thoughts, comparing her life with the lives of others and the treatment of others; instead she ought to use the high standards of revolution to measure her attitude toward the revolutionary line of Chairman Mao and her contribution to socialist construction. As a result she firmly resolved to teach her sons and daughters to put down roots in the villages.

Have Concern for the Parents   Resolve Difficulties

"The production of the masses, the well-being of the masses, the experiences of the masses, the feelings of the masses, the leading cadres should constantly notice all these things." The "Education Coordinating Group" followed this teaching of Chairman Mao and warmly concerned itself with the thought and life of every parent, helping the parents resolve real difficulties, and made progress in increasing the parents' sense of responsibility to teach their sons and daughters to engage in agriculture.

In October 1971, the educated youth Hsiao Pi, who had joined a brigade in Heilungkiang, was seriously injured while driving. When the "Education Coordinating Group" learned of this, it immediately sent off a telegram of consolation and organized the parents to be at Hsiao Pi's home through the night to comfort his parents and help look after his three younger brothers and sisters so that Hsiao Pi's parents could go without anxiety to Heilungkiang to look after him. When they learned that Hsiao Pi was returning to Shanghai to recuperate, these parents made arrangements with the hospital and made elaborate prep-

arations to receive him. While Hsiao Pi was in the hospital,
everyone went many times to visit him and take care of him
and also brought nutritous food to help him recuperate. Hsiao
Pi's parents said with feeling, "We have intimately felt the
warmth of the great revolutionary family; we have understood
the class feeling of revolutionary comrades!" Since then,
Hsiao Pi's parents frequently persuade other parents to mobilize and volunteer to do work in coordinating reeducation.

Voluntary Coordination   Educate the Youth

"The resettling area and the mobilizing town must coordinate
closely, support each other, work hard together, and do good
work." The "Education Coordinating Group," following this
spirit, voluntarily strengthened its ties with the resettling area
so that work of consolidating the movement up to the mountains
and down to the countryside became more and more firm.

In the past two years, they frequently wrote letters to the
concerned communes and brigades in each place to promote
relationships, coordinate with the masses of poor and lower-
middle peasants, and encourage young people to resolutely
walk upon the road of mutually uniting with the workers and
peasants. These places also wrote frequently, reporting on
the conditions of the young people being reeducated. The land
of the progressive production brigade of Huan-ta-ch'i Commune
in Heilungkiang was mountainous and forested. Some of the
educated youths who joined the brigade there began to fear
hardship. The "Education Coordinating Group" therefore organized some parents who had had deep and bitter experiences
in the old society to recollect the past and compare it with the
present; they recorded this and brought it to be played back for
the young people, so that they received a deep class education.
When the young people, under the stimulus of their parents,
compared themselves with their parents who had suffered
severe exploitation and oppression in the old society, they
realized that today there was incomparable good fortune, and
all said that they would not forget class bitterness and would

firmly recall with hatred the blood and tears that were shed. They resolved to set down roots in the mountain area village and struggle bitterly for a lifetime. Under the reeducation of the poor and lower-middle peasants, they brought their own understanding back to Shanghai. After the parents heard this, they deeply felt that although Shanghai and Heilungkiang are separated by several thousand li, as long as we strengthen our ties, the work of coordinating reeducation can be carried out very well.

The Kuei-chou neighborhood is situated in the center of the most prosperous part of Shanghai. Before liberation, the fresh blood of countless revolutionary martyrs flowed here; a glorious revolutionary tradition exists here. However, this area is also a place where dirt and filth were hidden beneath the surface. After liberation and the transformation following many political movements, Nanking East Road changed completely, so that there appeared heroic companies like the "Nanking East Road Good Eight Company," in which "a person can live in a noisy city, and remain unsullied." This gave the road much glory. This great socialist revolution of going up to the mountains and down to the countryside refreshed the atmosphere of Nanking Road. The revolutionary masses say: The movement of educated youths up to the mountains and down to the countryside is changing habits and customs, reconstructing the people's thinking and producing a new socialist atmosphere in which labor is important and aiding the peasants is glorious. Today everyone is concerned about rural affairs; everyone thinks what the poor and lower-middle peasants think. Everyone joins in educating one family's sons and daughters; one family has difficulties, everyone comes to help; this is the new spirit brought to us by the Proletarian Cultural Revolution!

Shanghai Revolutionary Committee
Down to the Countryside, Up to the
Mountains Office

9

Important Content of the Revolution in Education

Yenan Middle School Party Branch, Tientsin*

Among the students whom our school has graduated since 1968, more than thirteen hundred have gone to the villages and border regions to join the brigades and make a home. There they have been tempered and matured in the Three Great Revolutionary Movements in the villages. Not a few have become members of the Chinese Communist Party and the Communist Youth League. Many have joined the leadership ranks on varying levels or have undertaken technical work and have become very useful in the struggle to construct new socialist villages. These rich results have greatly encouraged the school's students, teachers and revolutionary parents, making the Party's educational policies enter their hearts more deeply, and making the idea that agricultural work is glorious pass from class to class. We have come to understand through practice that the

---

*T'ien-chin shih Yen-an chung-hsüeh tang chih-pu, "Chiao-yü ke-ming ti i-hsiang chung-yao nei-jung."

school must regard coordination with the villages in reeducating students who have gone to the countryside as an important aspect of the educational revolution.

In 1968 our great leader Chairman Mao announced that "educated youths must go to the countryside to be reeducated by the poor and lower-middle peasants." The students in the "three old classes" (that is, the classes of '66, '67, and '68) found that after the tempering of the Proletarian Cultural Revolution, the great majority of them had achieved a profound understanding of the meaning of Chairman Mao's directive. Resolved to carry it out, they went one after another to the villages. Under these circumstances, some of the teachers said, "Once we've seen the students out the door, our responsibilities are over. Their tempering is their own responsibility, no need for us to worry." Although the Party branch felt that this viewpoint was not quite right, it still did not pay enough attention to it. After a period of time, we heard that some of the students had met with some difficulties in the villages and were vacillating in their thought; and some individual students had also done some wrong things. At that time the whole school was discussing it, and not a few teachers held that we ought to form bonds with the villages and coordinate with the work of the poor and lower-middle peasants in ideological education; on the other hand, some people also held that the school is the agency that sends people, it is in charge of mobilization, and it is the poor and lower-middle peasants' business to educate them after they have reached the countryside; it is not necessary to be concerned with so many things.

Should we concern ourselves with this? Is it after all an "external" or an "internal" matter? Considering this question, we organized all the teachers to study conscientiously the Party directive on education, study the discussions of Chairman Mao relating to the cultivation of successors to the proletarian revolutionary cause, and criticize the crimes of swindlers like Liu Shao-ch'i who would destroy the educational revolution, so that everyone would understand that the proletarian educational revolution is a profound and great social revolution, and that among its important responsibilities is to teach the students to walk on the road of mutually uniting with the workers and peasants, and that its basic goal is to cultivate and create thousands of millions of successors to the proletarian revolutionary cause. Looking at it in the large context of revolution, education in school and reeducation after the students have left school are two intimately related factors in the process of cultivating successors to the revolution. Examining this from the reality of class struggle, we see that after the graduating students have gone to the countryside, they still maintain close connections with things, so that the thinking of the exploiting class in the towns and countryside still affects them: the residual poison of the revisionist educational line promoted by swindlers like Liu Shao-ch'i is still eroding them; a small number of class enemies are also falsely struggling to capture them. Because of this, the school should voluntarily help the poor and lower-middle peasants to do a good job in their work of reeducation, whether the help is given by means of letters to and from the students in the countryside, or whether it is given through their contacts when they return to the city and visit the school.

When we had clarified its significance, we developed this work by following different streams, grasping different kinds of opportunities, making use of methods such as going visiting and inviting people in, sending letters and study materials, and so on. Sixteen times in the past few years, we have sent out many different kinds of study and inquiry groups made up of representatives from the Party branch, the revolutionary committee, work and propaganda teams, teachers, and parents of students; we also sent more than five thousand letters and study materials. By these actions, the students sent to the countryside were greatly encouraged. They said, "What the comrades bring is not only the charges given us by the teachers and students of our alma mater, but also the warm concern of the four million people of Tientsin and the abundant hopes of the Party and of Chairman Mao."

What is the most important thing to grasp in coordinating reeducation? In the beginning we only grasped a few concrete problems relating to students who have gone to the countryside. Later, after undergoing study, we understood that we must not allow the attitude of "officials on a mission to the provinces" and "inspection" work to appear, but must ourselves be re-educated by the poor and lower-middle peasants together with the educated youths. At the same time we must actively coordinate with the poor and lower-middle peasants in carrying out ideological and political work with the students in the countryside, and help them to understand deeply the teaching of Chairman Mao that "the villages are a vast universe where one can be of great use." In this way they may unceasingly raise their willingness to be reeducated by the poor and lower-middle peasants, work hard to change their world view, and fully develop their usefulness. Once when a student did something wrong after he was in the countryside, we worked with the poor and lower-middle peasants to help him use Marxism-Leninism-Mao Tsetung Thought to analyze the causes and lessons of his wrongdoing; we encouraged him to put down his burden and, traveling light, become advanced. After a period of tempering, this student changed greatly and became actively useful in digging wells to protect against drought and in supplementary production, receiving good comments from the masses. Not long afterward he joined with honor the Communist Youth League.

In coordinating reeducation, we also emphasized understanding some of the ways in which the thinking of students who have gone to the countryside can change. We must not miss the opportunity of coordinating our work with the poor and lower-middle peasants when conditions are bitter, or the situation changes, or difficulties are met, or problems arise on holidays. The living conditions in the Heng-shui area of Hopei are relatively harsh; the students who have graduated from our school each year have gathered mainly in this area to join brigades and make homes. In order to encourage the students to become tempered and matured in harsh and rough surroundings, we have sent out small inquiry groups five times to visit the ten or so brigades that make up the four communes in this area, to coordinate their work with the ideological and political work of the poor and lower-middle peasants, and to help the students gradually make firm their resolution to set down roots in Heng-shui to carry out revolution. While visiting in the Heilung Harbor work area, many students excitedly declared that they wanted to be united together with the poor and lower-middle peasants always, to work hard and quickly at emulating Tachai, vowing that Heng-shui would change to be like Kiang-nan [south of the Yangtze]. Each time the students in the countryside return to Tientsin for a holiday or for some business, we always strive to "invite them in," to sit down and discuss with us what they have learned from their reeducation, help them to summarize and elevate it in order to develop their usefulness in the vast universe of the villages. On each national day, on New Year's, and on commemorative days, we always mobilize the teachers and students of the entire school to write solicitous letters to the students who have gone to the countryside, and to send them study materials. At ordinary times, we also use the exchange of letters to understand their situation, to communicate our thoughts, and to encourage each other. Many students in the countryside say in their return letters, "Although we are many hundreds of miles from our alma mater, our hearts and the hearts of the teachers and students of the entire school are very closely tied together." Once we discovered from a letter that someone who had been a student member of the school revolutionary committee had experienced some depression after he went to the countryside because of difficulties he met with in a collective household. The Party branch and revolutionary committee took the lead in writing opportune letters to encourage him to conquer these difficulties and to run the youth's collective household well. With the support of the poor and lower-middle peasants, he and his classmates united in struggle and finally conquered the difficulties so that the collective household changed and acquired a new appearance.

In coordinating reeducation, we chiefly coordinate our work in ideological education. Insofar as possible we actively help the poor and lower-middle peasants in the hsien and communes to satisfactorily solve concrete problems that are reported about students in the countryside. Problems that cannot be resolved at the time are reported to the leadership at higher levels and to the relevant agencies.

Among the students who have gone to the countryside from our school in these years, many have emerged as progressives. We use their progressive aspects as teaching materials, especially in teaching about engaging in agriculture. In addition, we have made this type of education a regular feature. The concept that engaging in agriculture is glorious is passed on from class to class in our school. A few days ago, during the mobilization meeting for going up to the mountains and down to the countryside, more than forty students declared that they want to learn from the alumni, and like them stand up and let the Party select them, take the lead in making revolution by going up to the mountains and down to the countryside, and resolutely walk the road of mutual unity with workers and peasants. After the meeting, the entire school became a hot tide of volunteering to go up to the mountains and down to the countryside.

The student Hsü Fu-shun, after he had put down his name, actively propagandized his whole family on the concept that engaging in agriculture is glorious; he received the support of his whole family and they actively prepared his luggage for him and saw him off. The atmosphere on the day when the school held its meeting to see the students off to the mountains and countryside was even more moving. The parent of student Yuan Chin-jung quickly hurried to the meeting after he got off work from the late shift and sincerely asked the school leadership to allow his daughter to go to the countryside to engage in agriculture. Chao Kuei-ch'in, deputy secretary of the school League main branch and graduating student in this class, even brought together more than twenty students and organized a Long March Brigade for going up to the mountains and down to the countryside. They walked to Pao-ti hsien to join the brigades and make homes. After they reached the countryside, the graduates received the warm welcome of the village Party organization and the poor and lower-middle peasants.

10

As the Party Nurtured Me, So Will I Nurture the Educated Youths

Su Le-wen*

Encouraged by the admonition of our great leader Chairman Mao that "educated youths must go to the villages to be re-educated by the poor and lower-middle peasants.... Comrades in villages everywhere should welcome their going," we at Nan-sa Brigade in I-ch'eng <u>hsien</u>, Shansi, welcomed twenty-three educated youths who came to the countryside from Peking in December 1968.

Reeducation of educated youths is for the purpose of nurturing and creating successors to the proletarian revolutionary cause and quickening the construction of new socialist villages; it is also a glorious political responsibility which the Party and Chairman Mao have given to us basic-level cadres and poor and lower-middle peasants. We must carry this heavy responsibility

---

*Su Le-wen (Secretary of the Party Branch of Nan-sa Brigade, I-ch'eng <u>Hsien</u>), "Tang tsen-yang p'ei-yang wo, wo chiu p'ei-yang chih-shih ch'ing-nien."

93

with self-awareness and earnestly do a good job of administering education to the educated youths. We cadres on the basic
level in the villages have all gradually matured under the nurturing education of the Party. Thinking back on my own case,
in these more than thirty years the Party organization has constantly been concerned about me, has looked after me, has educated me, has spent no one knows how much time, work, and
money on me, to bring me up from an ignorant youth to a basic-
level cadre in the Party. Whenever I recall these things, I feel
deeply that to put into practice the revolutionary line of Chairman Mao and to cultivate successors to the revolution are related to the important questions of whether or not the proletarian revolution will have successors and whether or not our
Party and our country will change color. Because of these re-
flections, in the past years I have worked with educated youths
and earnestly nurtured them just as the Party has nurtured me.

As the Party Educated Me, So Will I Patiently Educate the Educated Youths

When the educated youths first arrived in the villages, the
masses of poor and lower-middle peasants were happy and
warmly welcomed them. However, there were also a few cadres and people whose understanding was not correct and who
felt that their arrival was merely a nuisance and was hard to
manage. A member of the Party branch said to me, "These
kids, they're educated and always up to something; we rough
folks won't be able to manage them." At that time, I felt that
that kind of talk was not right, but I couldn't give a reason for
it. To resolve the matter, I repeatedly studied the discussions
of Chairman Mao that concern the work of young people, and I
understood that the young people dare to think, dare to speak,
and dare to do; they have a fresh spirit, but they are still not
mature, they lack experience; by correctly leading them and
patiently teaching them, their value can be nurtured. Thinking
back, I remember that when I first joined in revolutionary work,
I too was an ignorant youth and did not understand the meaning

of class and revolution; I only thought that "poverty and wealth are determined by fate." The Party organization talked to me about revolution and I came to understand that poor people had to unite to make revolution in order to reverse things and achieve liberation. Under the leadership of the Party, I joined the people's militia, joined the Peasants' Association, acted as courier, struggled with the landlords, and together with the masses, actively expanded the struggle against the enemy. One day in 1942, the Japanese enemy had surrounded our village and killed fourteen soldiers. At that time I was both grieved and angry, but I didn't know what to do. At that key juncture, the Party organization sent people to our village to organize the masses. They spoke to us about such revolutionary principles as "difficulties are temporary, victory is just ahead." It was like parting the black clouds and seeing the sun; we all clearly understood the direction of struggle and became firm in our belief that the revolution would certainly be victorious. Thinking of the nurturing and the education that the Party gave me, and relating it to working with educated youths, I advanced a step in understanding that it was only with Chairman Mao's leadership and the nurturing of the Party that today's situation is possible. In order to raise the sense of responsibility of the masses of cadres and poor and lower-middle peasants toward the nurturing and education of educated youths, I organized everyone to study the works of Chairman Mao; I used my own case of being educated by the Party when I was young and subsequently finding the revolutionary path as an example so that everyone would have a better understanding that reeducating the masses of educated youths is a responsibility that we cannot refuse as a matter of principle. Many of our comrades are people like myself; they too grew up under the nurturing and education of the Party; everyone understood. Thus we very quickly agreed, and resolved to attack the problem vigorously and cultivate the educated youths in the countryside so that they would become successors to the proletarian revolutionary cause.

How should reeducation of educated youths be carried out? I deeply understood from my own education by the Party that, first, class education must be carried out, that consciousness of the line must be raised through study of the basics. We could walk in a relatively resolute manner upon the road of revolution when we were young because of this principle. To enable the educated youths to become successors to the revolution today, we must also begin with class education. Thus our Party branch mobilized the masses of people to carry out class education, line education, and revolutionary tradition education among the educated youths. We talked to them about the three histories*, organized them to eat "recalling-bitterness" meals, hold recalling bitterness meetings, visit the laborer's caves, and visit the monuments of martyrs, so that they would receive a profound education about classes and the revolutionary tradition. In the past, the poor peasant Han Hsüeh-jen lived in a laborer's cave and, because the cave had no door, his wife was eaten by a wolf; the poor peasant Su Kuang-ch'i had a father who, because the landlord was dunning him over a debt, hanged himself on the last day of the year in the laborer's cave; and early in 1942, Su Kuang-ch'i and others, fourteen comrades in all, were killed by the enemy while taking part in our village's unyielding underground work, thus dying a martyr's death for the revolution. The class hatred and feelings of revenge related one after another greatly stimulated the class feeling of the educated youths in the countryside and raised their consciousness of line struggle, so that they resolved to set down roots in the villages to make revolution as the revolutionaries had done a generation before them.

Ideological education is not a one-time thing; the thinking of the educated youths can sometimes also suffer relapses. For this reason, it is necessary to firmly and unceasingly work with them. Last year when the brigade selected two educated youths to go to the factories to become workers, the event caused some educated youths to vacillate in their thinking. They felt that "a worker has a future; being left behind in the villages is so unpromising." In response to this type of incorrect think-

---

*See the Glossary.

ing, I talked to them about an experience from my own past: after the whole country was liberated, some people tried to persuade me to go outside to work. I thought, agriculture is the
basis, the revolution needs me to remain in the villages to work
in agricultural production. In these twenty years and more,
from the period of the mutual-aid teams and the elementary cooperative to today's people's commune, I have remained in the
villages, working with the poor and lower-middle peasants
against the elements and changing the appearance of the villages; in addition several times I have attended provincial, local and hsien model worker meetings and received public praise
of the Party and the people; how can anyone say that it is "unpromising" to be in the villages?

The young people, seeing us basic-level cadres and poor and
lower-middle peasants bitterly struggle for several decades in
the villages and make revolution without any other desire, slowly
became clearer in their thinking. They resolutely declared:
"Our red hearts are given to the Party; our lives will follow the
arrangements made by the Party." The educated youth Wang
Ch'un-fu was originally restless in the village but after he
understood the relationship between staying and leaving he made
up his mind to set down roots for a lifetime in the village and
give all his energy to the construction of new socialist villages.
He voluntarily enrolled to work at the San-yen-kou Reservoir
five li away from the village. For more than a year now, he has
been living in the mountain valley, taking care of the canals and
at the same time cutting grass to feed the collective's pigs, and
he is praised by the masses.

As the Party Was Concerned About Me, So Will I
Show Warm Concern for the Educated Youths

At the same time that we are educating the educated youths,
we must also earnestly find good solutions to their concrete
living problems, such as food, housing, clothing, health care,
and so on. A good resolution of these problems will even better

help them to set down roots in the villages to make revolution.
In the beginning, we did not all have the same understanding of
this problem. For example, take the question of building housing. Some of the cadres felt that we should build no more houses
for the educated youths than those for which the higher levels
had allocated money. Others also suggested that we shouldn't
invest too much in them, enough to get by would be fine. Whether
just to get by, or to resolve the problem conscientiously was a
very important question. Remembering the concern that the
Party had shown me on the question of living needs for the last
few decades caused me to understand that a warm concern for
the problems of the livelihood of the educated youths is an important condition for their healthy growth. In the period of resisting the Japanese, I once went through a rainstorm to bring
back some intelligence and suddenly became very sick and had
a high fever; for several days I was unconscious. Because at
that time the Japanese devils were blockading the area to make
a sweep through it, my family had no money at home and no way
to buy medicine. When the Party organization learned of this,
they sent medicine under very difficult circumstances and with
much planning, so that I could recover. Several decades have
passed, but whenever I remember that incident, my heart warms.
Now Chairman Mao has given us the responsibility of nurturing
the educated youths; how can we consider only the economic account? What about the political debt? I talked to everyone about
this, and the poor and lower-middle peasants and the masses of
commune members all declared: "We must do our utmost to
solve the housing and other concrete living problems of the educated youths." With our thinking straightened out, our actions
became more self-determined. In 1969, in addition to the
amount allotted by the country for building housing, we ourselves also made more than 700,000 chin of lime, baked
more than 100,000 bricks, and quarried more than 100 pieces
of stone. In 1,500 work hours, we built for the educated youths
ten caves lined with bricks and five tiled houses. Twenty-three
educated youths thus had homes in which to sleep, kitchens in
which to eat, and storerooms in which to put grains and vegetables.

We have given suitable attention to the question of food for the educated youths. In the past four years, whether the harvest was rich or poor, the standard of their food has always remained at a level that is not lower than the standard for other individual local workers. We guarantee that they eat well and not go hungry. Satisfied, they say, "We have vegetables, we have white flour, at New Year's and special festivals we often have even better food; the cadres look after us, the commune members ask after us; the more we do, the more enthusiasm we have." In order that the educated youths achieve self-sufficiency and show a surplus in their livelihood, we frequently tell them of the principle that only by widely developing collective production and increasing the collective harvest is it possible to unceasingly raise the level of living, thus fully stimulating their activism for participating in collective production labor. The questions of livelihood settled, we also taught them how to live without waste. In these past few years, the educated youths in our brigade have not only achieved self-sufficiency in their living needs, but most of them have shown a surplus.

Our brigade put into practice a system of cooperative health care. The minor and light illnesses of the educated youths are treated on the spot; for the major and serious illnesses, we send them to the hospital. The cost of that is supplemented according to the situation. For those with chronic illnesses, we make suitable accommodations for their living needs and assign them to appropriate agricultural work. When the educated youth Hsiao Chiang was sick and could not do heavy work, we treated him for his illness and at the same time arranged for him to do some light work. Later he slowly took a turn for the better and his body became strong. When the brigade was repairing the reservoir, he even voluntarily put his name down for the work. The educated youth Hsiao Yin contracted inflammation of the lung tissue, lymphatic tuberculosis, and other illnesses. Because the local hospital conditions were insufficient, the brigade sent her back to Peking for treatment. During her period of treatment, besides writing continuously to ask after her, we also supplied her food ration. This attention made Hsiao Yin

and her entire family feel deeply moved; even before she was
completely cured, she brought some medicine with her and returned to the brigade to actively participate in labor.

In the course of doing this training and educating work, I
came to understand that warm concern for the lives of the educated youths cannot be just passively supplying food and drink,
but must include actively nurturing good habits of hard struggle.
On National Day in 1970, they held a discussion and then killed
one of the fat pigs they were breeding, went into town and bought
many foodstuffs, prepared a large feast, and sat down to a
hearty meal. When we discovered this matter, we talked to
them about the time the elementary cooperatives were first set
up. At that time, the foundation was thin, and the livestock weak;
in order to increase the livestock, everyone braved the wind and
snow to go up to the mountains, taking dried foods with them.
On the mountains they did auxiliary work, carrying coal on their
shoulders. Sometimes they didn't eat a good meal for one or
two days. It was by a winter of this kind of harsh work that they
bought three head of livestock, thus advancing the spring planting and production. After the educated youths heard this, they
realized that both their thinking and actions were wrong and,
except for some which they kept, sold the greater part of the
meat to the state, and spent the holiday in a revolutionary style.

Our Party branch also mobilized the masses of poor and
lower-middle peasants to tell them and demonstrate to them
many things. They helped them work and study; they taught
them to make their own shoes and clothing and to live economically. Nowadays, those young girls all make their own shoes
when their shoes wear out, and mend their own clothes when
they are torn. They also make much clothing for their families
and for the poor and lower-middle peasants. Besides this, we
also lead them in feeding the pigs and raising chickens and in
opening up uncultivated land to plant grain and vegetables. In
these years, they have fed 8 pigs, raised 105 chickens, and harvested 2,000 chin of grain and more than 5,200 chin of vegetables.
The increase in the harvest, the decrease in expenditure, the good
management of living needs — these enabled the educated youths to
settle better in the villages without worry.

As the Party Used Me, So Will I Boldly
Use the Educated Youths

In order to nurture the educated youths in the countryside to become successors to the proletarian revolutionary cause, it is necessary to let them experience winds and rains, see the world and be tempered in the Three Great Revolutionary Movements, and to let them increase their abilities through practice and grow healthily through struggle.

We also struggled ideologically over the question of whether or not we dared to use the educated youths boldly. In the autumn of 1970, there were three educated youths who separately took on the responsibilities of secretary of the brigade League branch, team custodian, and leader of a production team. Most of the cadres and poor and lower-middle peasants were very approving. They said to the educated youths, "Do the work well; we stand by you." However, there was also a minority of cadres and commune members who were uneasy. They said to me, "Old secretary, we have been a progressive brigade for many years; with these kids as cadres, what will we do if they mess it up?" Hearing this feedback, I again remembered something from twenty or more years ago: in the spring of 1952, when we set up the first elementary agricultural producers' cooperative in the entire hsien, the people chose me to be the leader of the cooperative. Some people said with concern, "Le-wen is still young; can he shoulder such a heavy responsibility?" I was also very timid in my heart, afraid that I wouldn't be able to do much. It was at that point that the hsien notified me to attend a special district meeting; I went and met the higher-level leadership. I reported my thinking and they warmly encouraged me, saying, "Work boldly. Ability is acquired by learning, competence is acquired by practice. If you obey the Party and consult the people when things come up, you will certainly manage the cooperative well." After the meeting, the hsien committee also sent a responsible comrade to our village to help manage the cooperative. If I didn't know how to mobilize the masses, he would teach me; if I didn't understand the techniques of agricultural science,

he would introduce me to some outside place where I could
visit and learn; if I didn't know some words, he would patiently
teach me culture. Under the leadership of the Party, the cooperative was managed better and better so that in the first year
grain and cotton production was greatly increased. It was in
the course of that kind of struggle that I slowly acquired some
competence in working for the people. This made me understand that a person cannot become steel without a hundred temperings and cannot become timber without experiencing winds
and rains. In this way the Party selflessly nurtured me and
boldly used me. We must also have full confidence in the educated youths, use them boldly, and nurture them to become successors to the proletarian revolutionary cause by placing them
at the peak of the waves and the funnel of the wind in class
struggle, production struggle, and scientific experimentation.
Ruminating on these matters, I called a cadre meeting and a
mass meeting, and organized everyone to review and study the
great teaching of Chairman Mao that "the successors to the
proletarian revolutionary cause are born in the struggle of the
masses, are matured by the temperings of the great winds and
waves of the revolution." All raised their level of understanding, and agreement in thought was achieved. Everyone declared:
"We must boldly use the educated youths." Thus twelve educated
youths at one time or another took up the responsibility of being
cadres in the brigade and in production teams. After assuming
this heavy responsibility, they took the lead in working bitterly
and hard, their hearts completely in the collective. After the
young girl Han Hsüeh-ch'in became leader of the women's team,
she became even more energetic in her work and even more
concerned. Last year when she went home to visit her family
for the New Year, her body was in Peking but her heart was in
Nan-sa; her vacation was not yet up when she returned early to
the brigade to take part in the production work of spring planting.

   While using the young people, we still firmly continue to
carry out nurturing education. After the educated youth Li Ching-
jung became the leader of the women's team in the production

team, she was very enthusiastic and willing to do everything, but she lacked work skills. Last year, during the "three summer months," she led the women to the fields to hoe corn. A girl refused to work after being called several times; she even said, "I'm not going to do any work. What's that to do with you?" Li Ching-jung was very angry when she heard this and came to look for me and refused to be brigade leader no matter what I said. So I showed her how to do ideological work and encouraged her not to fear being snubbed. Little Li made up her mind to do good work, and many times she went to the home of that commune member and discovered that the reason she did not work hard was that she had many children and tiring household duties. The difficulties were real. Li Ching-jung, while helping her raise her consciousness, found the time to help her sew and mend clothing, husk rice and grind wheat, lightening her household responsibilities so that she voluntarily joined in collective productive labor.

In the course of boldly using and educating the educated youths, all of us members of the Party branch were very conscious of setting examples ourselves, of talking with words and showing by actions, so that we might become models for them. Once when we were building a dam to control the river at Hai-tzu-kou north of the village, there was a sudden rainstorm and the water rose very high. It looked as though the dam would burst before our eyes. At that key point a few of the branch committee members and I were the first to jump into the water; the educated youths then also jumped into the water. The flood waters knocked them down, but they got up and continued to work; the tumbling rocks bruised their feet and legs, but they refused to make a sound. I tried to persuade them to get up onto the shore, but they resolutely said, "If you don't get up, we won't get up either. Whatever you do, we'll do!" After more than four hours, we were victorious over the flood waters and were able to save the dam. This real situation has caused us to understand profoundly that in bringing up the educated youths the cadres must set the example. If we lead them on the correct road, the educated youths will grow quickly.

"The villages are a vast universe where one can be of great use." After four years of tempering, the educated youths of our brigade are now growing healthily. Among them, two have already gloriously joined the Chinese Communist Party, fifteen have joined the Communist Youth League, and nine have been sent to different battle lines. The educated youths sent to the countryside have developed great usefulness in the Three Great Revolutionary Movements and have already become an indispensable and newborn force in the socialist revolution and socialist construction of the villages.

11

Teaching by Word and Deed,
Lead the New Troops Well

Wei Chiang-ko*

Since 1970, a total of forty-six educated urban youths have come to our Kuo-li Brigade in I-shan hsien, Kwangsi Province, to become members of the brigade and establish residence. In the past, when I was a squad leader in the army, for five years I led a squad of soldiers who were breaking down mountains and constructing a road on the high plateau of Tibet. Now Chairman Mao is calling on educated youth to go up to the mountains and down to the countryside to unite with the workers and peasants. When they arrive in the village, I am as happy as I was in those years when I welcomed new troops. I am determined to go into battle with this group of new warriors to construct new mountain areas so that Chairman Mao and other elders need not worry. For over two years now the poor and lower-middle

---

*Wei Chiang-ko (Assistant Party Branch Secretary of Kuo-li Brigade, I-shan Hsien), "Yen-ch'uan shen-chiao, tai-hao hsin ping."

peasants and I have taught the educated youths by word and deed. We have warmly helped and led them, making possible their healthy growth and fostering their active usefulness in the Three Great Revolutionary Movements in the villages.

I

Our brigade is one with high mountains and few fields in the Chuang Nationality mountain country. When some of the educated youths arrive here and see endless mountains and valleys, they are speechless; and because life is comparatively difficult, their thoughts begin to waver. I think it not so strange that city youths' thoughts vacillate when they first arrive in mountainous areas. It is mainly because they have been poisoned by revisionist education and have an incorrect understanding of ideals and the course of the future. After studying the situation, the Party committee let me form a study group with the youths to study Chairman Mao's instruction that "the villages are a vast universe where one can be of great use" and other lessons. I discussed with them the ideals and future of youth and fiercely criticized the theory spread by swindlers like Liu Shao-ch'i that the mountain areas are backward. I discussed with them the time the People's Liberation Army was constructing the road in Tibet and indicated that the soldiers thought with one heart: "Where Chairman Mao points, there we will break through the mountains and open a road; everything for the victory of the revolution, for opening the road to prosperity for the Tibetan people, for the great task of building communism." These were our lofty proletarian ideals. The "theory that mountain areas are backward" spread by swindlers like Liu Shao-ch'i is a rash plan to incite us to leave the mountain areas and destroy socialist construction there. I also introduced them to the moving events in a production team in Pei-chiao that changed a poor mountain gulch that had to rely on state aid for grain and funds into a new mountain village which is more than self-sufficient in grain and in which the livelihood of the commune members improves daily. This was to illustrate that mountain areas are not without a future, but are where great deeds can be done. The changes in a mountain area helped them realize the reality of the struggle between two lines and motivated them to be like the People's Liberation Army and rush wherever Chairman Mao points, always taking the revolutionary road indicated by Chairman Mao.

When the educated youth Hsiao Pao returned home to visit her family and saw that some of her classmates were factory workers and some were teachers, she began to think that her own work in the mountain valleys held little promise for the future, and her morale fell. I entered her door to find her and have a heart-to-heart talk, and especially to present her with a pair of straw sandals. I said to her: "The Red Army wore them when they completed the Long March with Chairman Mao; the people's sons in the army wore them when they were breaking through mountains and opening a road to Lhasa in Tibet. Today, when you are wearing them in the rural villages, you must follow to the end the revolutionary road indicated by Chairman Mao." She took the straw sandals and said with tears in her eyes, "I will certainly learn from the former revolutionary generation and rush wherever Chairman Mao points. There will I put down roots, blossom, and produce fruit." After her understanding was elevated, Hsiao Pao enthusiastically fought in the front line of the Three Great Revolutionary Movements with the poor and lower-middle peasants.

In November 1971, Hsiao Pao, working with male commune members at a water conservancy site, sank a sand extractor over ten meters into a mountain cave. The cave was so dark that they had to use a mirror to reflect the sunlight, and at night they had to light a fire to work. For more than ten successive days Hsiao Pao worked in the icy water and did not leave the firing line. During the 1972 battle to protect the early seedlings, Hsiao Pao fought day and night for over thirty days without talking about difficulty or fatigue and won the warm praise of the poor and lower-middle peasants. Hsiao Pao resolutely indicated to the Party branch that she would not be moved by wind or waves in putting down roots in the mountain areas to make revolution.

II

Our great leader Chairman Mao has taught us that "the construction of a socialist system has opened a road for us that
will extend to the limit of our ideals, but the realization of this
ideal limit depends on our industrious labor." Educated youths
are enthusiastic and accept new things rather quickly, but because they lack tempering in the Three Great Revolutionary
Movements, their thinking about many situations is very simpli stic
and rather easily begins to waver when they meet with difficult
work. When they first arrived they feared the excrement and
the smell when they carried night soil, they feared hardship and
fatigue when they went to the fields. When the poor and lower-
middle peasants went into the valleys to work, carrying on their
backs scythes, bamboo containers and gourds full of water, the
youths thought it looked queer and did not want to do it. This is
because they lacked the thought and feelings of the poor and
lower-middle peasants. To help the students transform their
idealism for building up the mountain areas into voluntary revolutionary action, I taught them the proletarian revolutionary
soldier's morality of our revolutionary forebears who did not
fear hardship or death, who considered hardship to be glorious
and joyful. I regularly told them of moving incidents that occurred when the People's Liberation Army was constructing the
road in Tibet. The People's Liberation Army broke through
mountains and opened a road over five thousand meters up on
the Tibetan high plateau in order to liberate the suffering agricultural slaves and strengthen our national borders. The air
was very thin and snow piled up in the winter. They braved bitter cold as they blasted holes in the overhanging cliffs and steep
walls. Their hands and feet cracked in the cold and fresh blood
oozed onto their faces and their tools, but no one complained.
Rather, they magnanimously said "The bitterness of this labor
is sweet to our hearts; we will eat all the bitterness in the world
to realize the communist course." Almost every foot of earth on
that 2,250 kilometer road is washed with the blood and sweat of
heroes. Encouraged by the heroic deeds of their revolutionary

forebears, the youths decided to sharpen their revolutionary
wills in that difficult environment and temper themselves to
become revolutionary descendants who can eat much bitterness
and endure great labor.

In the winter of 1971, they were repairing the village reservoir. One day, just as everyone was at the base of the surrounding ditch, a leak was suddenly discovered at the bottom of the
dike, threatening the safety of the volunteer workers at the base.
It had to be stopped up immediately. Wang Jen-pao and three
other educated youths leaped one after another into the water
to repair the leaking hole. The river water was bone-chilling,
and after working for a while they would come back up to get
warm. They struggled for two hours, going up and down four
times. They said with determination: "We have learned from
our revolutionary forebears that in the difficult struggle to construct new mountain areas, cold water warms the heart!"

To go a step further in educating the youths to carry on difficult struggle, I often focused on the reality of their thought by
discussing with them the history of how the poor and lower-
middle peasants changed their lives [fan-shen]. Once I took the
educated youth Ai Tsu-yu to learn how to harrow a field. He
was wearing shoes and socks which he took off and put on the
embankment when he reached the field. Because the weather
was a little cold, he went down to the field and then ran back
up three times. Time and again I encouraged him to raise his
courage and struggle to overcome difficulties. I also helped
him dress properly for harrowing and to pull the row in front
of him. The fourth time little Ai went down to the field, he
stayed there. That evening I invited little Ai and three other
educated youths to my home. I took out my "common laborer's
carrying pole" and told them my family history. I said: "In the
old society I used this carrying pole from age sixteen, giving a
landlord over ten years of my life. I don't know how much blood
and sweat was pressed out of me by the landlord. The bitterness
of those times is incalculable. When I returned from the army
to the village, I again used this 'common laborer's carrying
pole' to break up the mountains and open the summits with the

masses of commune members. I carried dirt to create fields
and transform the backward appearance of Pei-chiao. A load
of a thousand chin didn't seem difficult, the weight on my shoulder was sweetness in my heart! I want to use this carrying pole
right down to the realization of communism."

After they had listened, they were all moved to assert that
"sweetness comes from bitterness; how can there be sweetness
without bitterness? To construct a new socialist countryside,
we must struggle hard in the rural villages for a lifetime."
These educated youths regularly took turns using my carrying
pole to do heavy and dirty work.

Once little Ai and some commune members were hauling gypsum from twenty li [about seven miles] away on Ou-t'ung Road.
He had planned to eat his noon meal on the road, but by chance
the restaurant on that road was closed that day. Little Ai
thought, "How will I have the strength to carry this load if I do
not eat?" But looking at the "common laborer's carrying pole"
in his hand aroused his courage, and he continued carrying the
gypsum back to the production team. The commune members
asked him if he was tired and he replied, "Carrying the 'common laborer's carrying pole' and planting the fields for revolution makes the pressure on my shoulders sweetness to my
heart."

III

I deeply believe that every boost and every shove by us poor
and lower-middle peasants can influence the development of educated youths who come to the villages to be reeducated. We
must make strict demands on ourselves in order truly to act as
examples for educated youths.

One day when I was taking a turn at turning and drying over
3,000 chin of maize that belonged to the team, my wife also carried over 50 chin of maize to dry in a corner of the drying area
and asked me to keep an eye on it too. At noon, it suddenly
started to rain. While I was carrying the team's maize into the
storage area, my own maize was washed by the rain into a

gutter by the side of the drying area. This event provided much inductive education for the educated youths. In the 1972 summer harvest, Wei Ying-chiao, an educated girl, volunteered to turn and dry the team's maize. That day she carried out 6,000 chin of maize and divided it into two areas to dry. In the afternoon the weather suddenly changed and a heavy rain threatened. She quickly piled up the grain and called commune members who were working nearby to come and help. A commune member said that her own maize had not been collected and told her to do it quickly. "There is much grain that belongs to the collective. If it is soaked by the rain, the loss will be great. My little bit of maize does not matter!" While she talked she continued gathering and carrying the collective's maize. She carried thirty-six successive loads and just as it was all gathered in, the rain began to fall. Later, an older woman, seeing such wholehearted devotion to the collective, helped her collect the maize. When the poor and lower-middle peasants praised Wei Ying-chiao's spirit of warm love for the collective she said: "This is what Chiang-ko and the poor and lower-middle peasants taught me to do."

One spring there was a severe drought and 250 mou of fields in Pei-chiao Production Team lacked water and the young rice shoots could not be transplanted. Some people said: "We must bail water into this and that dry plot, if it doesn't rain soon, it's trouble we have got." After the team cadres and I studied the situation we raised the slogan "To fight the drought we'll try our hardest, we'll protect the seedlings and have a great harvest," and took the lead in drawing water, bailing water, carrying fertilizer and transplanting shoots with great energy. After thirty successive days and nights of bitter warfare, we transplanted the rice seedlings in time. In this struggle to combat the drought and transplant the seedlings, each educated youth strove to be first and battled in the front line. When the late rice crop was seriously attacked by pests, they actively participated day and night to eliminate them. Because they did so in time and saved the crop, there was good early and late rice harvests totaling over 65,000 chin. The total grain production for

the whole brigade increased 540,000 chin over 1971. These accomplishments are the result of the guidance provided by the
revolutionary line of Chairman Mao and the energetic struggle
of the cadres and commune members, and they cannot be separated from the strong efforts of the educated youths.

IV

Chairman Mao has taught us: "Educated youths must go to the
villages and receive reeducation from the poor and lower-middle
peasants.... Comrades from villages everywhere should welcome their going." It shows the greatest trust in us poor and lower-
middle peasants that Chairman Mao has given the educated
youths to us. We must treat them as our own sons and daughters,
have a warm concern for them so that they can make revolution
in the villages without worrying and will serve the poor and
lower-middle peasants with all their hearts and all their minds.

Each time educated youths arrive, the poor and lower-middle
peasants and I sweep out their dwellings, make their beds, and
provide tools for working and implements for living. If they are
not in the habit of participating in labor, we take them by the
hand and teach them, and gradually they become tempered. When
they get sick, I personally give them medicine, call the doctor,
and regularly go to visit them. I also tell my daughter to help
them carry water and cook. To make it convenient for them to
work, I find the time to give them straw sandals, scythes, and
wicker baskets. If they have no vegetables to eat and have no
container on the floor for hauling water, the poor and lower-
middle peasants and I supply them. If when they have just arrived they have no water crock I give them the rice crock from
my home to haul water in. I make every effort to prevent their
feeling difficulties in their livelihood. The educated youths are
very moved when they see the concern and consideration we
poor and lower-middle peasants have for them. They say: "The
poor and lower-middle peasants are closer than even our fathers
and mothers; Kuo-li Brigade is warmer than even our homes."
They have established deep proletarian feelings with the poor

and lower-middle peasants. They do everything they can to
help the poor and lower-middle peasants when they have difficulties. The educated youths buy Chairman Mao's books with
money they have saved and give them to the poor and lower-
middle peasants to study. They buy them medicines to cure
their illnesses. Under the leadership of the Party branch they
have motivated the masses to run a political and cultural night
school where they actively tutor the commune members in the
study of works by Marx, Lenin and Mao, and teach them to
study cultural subjects. Since 1972 our brigade has organized
the masses to study the "Communist Manifesto." They teach
the commune members to read each word and each sentence
and, hand holding hand, they teach them to write. Many commune members can now remember the basic points in the
"Communist Manifesto." Furthermore, using the viewpoint of
the "two breakaways" [chüeh-lieh] as a weapon, they have
changed some old habits.

Wei Feng-mei, a female commune member, used to be uncul-
tured. She had difficulty studying revolutionary theory. The
educated youths Pao Wang-mei and Wei Ping-hsing regularly
helped her study. Now Wei Feng-mei not only has a lower elementary school cultural level, she can also study revolutionary
theory and has raised her consciousness of class struggle and
line struggle. She has been chosen by the masses to be assistant battalion commander in the brigade militia.

When I see the great progress that the educated youths have
made under the education of the poor and lower-middle peasants and following the revolutionary line of Chairman Mao, I
am happy beyond words. In the past two years or so I have led
"new soldiers" for the revolution; and although I have done
some work, I have far from fulfilled the responsibility given me
by the Party. I am determined to avoid arrogance and impa-
tience and to do a still better job with educated youths who have
gone up to the mountains and down to the countryside. I will
contribute my full strength to cultivating successors to the proletarian revolutionary cause.

12

On the Question of Teaching Our Sons and Daughters
to Go down to the Countryside to Engage in Agriculture

Chao Heng-chang*

Under the guidance of Chairman Mao's proletarian revolutionary line, tens of millions of educated youths have enthusiastically responded to the call of the Party and have gone to our country's rural and border areas to take the revolutionary road of
uniting with workers and peasants. My heart is filled with hap-
piness when I see the vigorous growth of the younger generation.
Since 1962, I have followed the teachings of Chairman Mao,
and sent my children, one after the other, to the countryside to
weather the storm and face the world in the Three Great Revolutionary Movements. In over ten years of putting that principle into practice, I have felt deeply that the road of integration
with workers and peasants that my children are taking under
Chairman Mao's guidance is a revolutionary road for correcting
their world view, a fulfilling road of service to the people. Now
I want to discuss what I have learned from this experience of
sending sons and daughters to do farming in the countryside,

*Chao Heng-chang (member of the Shensi Party Committee
and a professor at the Northwest Agricultural Institute), "T'an-
t'an chiao tzu nü hsia-hsiang wu-nung ti wen-t'i."

so as to encourage other parents of educated youths.

Our great Chairman Mao has always concerned himself with the growth of young intellectuals. He pointed out in his famous lecture "The Direction of the Youth Movement" that "young intellectuals and students of the entire nation must unite with the masses of workers and peasants and become a single body with them." At the height of the collectivization of agriculture, he instructed that "whoever among the intellectuals can go to the villages to work should gladly go. The villages are a vast universe where one can be of great use." During the Proletarian Cultural Revolution, Chairman Mao again issued a great call, "Educated youths must go to the villages and receive reeducation from the poor and lower-middle peasants. We must persuade the cadres and others in the cities to send their sons and daughters who have graduated from lower-middle schools, upper-middle schools, and universities to the countryside and make it a campaign. Comrades from villages everywhere should welcome their going." This series of instructions from Chairman Mao not only clearly points out the direction in which all educated youths should go, but also points out to us parents the way to educate our sons and daughters. Because of this, whether or not parents support their sons and daughters going to the countryside to serve the peasants becomes a question of whether or not they put into practice the revolutionary road of Chairman Mao.

I was born into a family of the exploiting class. An intellectual from the old society, for more than thirty years I have been working with wheat seeds. Before liberation, I was under the influence of "Science to Save the Country" ideology, and motivated by the desire to find "a good seed to save the people," I separated myself from the masses of workers and peasants and engaged in individual struggle. I worked hard and produced "Pi-ma No. 1," a fine strain of wheat, but it was put into the "cold palace"* by the reactionary government of the Kuo-

---

*See the Glossary.

mintang, which ignored the life or death of the working people.
After liberation, the incomparably outstanding socialist system
has opened limitless prospects for scientific research in the
country. Under the concerned education of the Party, I have
steadfastly walked on the road of uniting with workers and peasants that Chairman Mao has indicated, and have made friends
with the poor, and lower-middle peasants, gone to the villages
for tempering through labor, corrected my world view, and
produced a few results in the work of cultivating seeds. Although this is nothing more than what a science worker ought to
do, the Party and the people have given me great honors. Since
1950 I have had the good fortune to meet our great leader Chairman Mao ten times. A special occasion was in 1957, when I
heard Chairman Mao's important talk "On The Correct Handling
of Contradictions among the People." I was profoundly educated
and to this day cannot forget it. From my personal experience,
I learned that only by listening to the words of Chairman Mao
and uniting with the workers and peasants can an intellectual
do something useful for the Party and the people; otherwise,
nothing will be accomplished. I also gradually came to understand that if an intellectual does not steadfastly participate in
collective labor, he cannot become one with the workers and
peasants, he cannot have the thoughts and emotions of the working people, so he cannot serve the people very well.

Under the influence of the above thinking, in 1962 I sent my
eldest son, Chao Pi, who had graduated from normal school, to
my hometown, Wu-chai Brigade, Chi hsien, Honan Province,
to be a peasant; in 1965 I sent my eldest daughter, Chao Liu who
had graduated from middle school to Wu-kung hsien, Li-ch'en
Brigade, for training; in 1968 I sent my second son, Chao
Hsiang, to Tai-chia Brigade, Wu-kung hsien, to receive reeducation from the poor and lower-middle peasants; in 1969 my
third son also went to the same group as Chao Hsiang, to settle.
Chao Liu later became a teacher in a popularly managed
school; the third son, after a period of learning through labor
in the village, was transferred to become a factory worker.
My actions thus do not mean that our sons and daughters can

only go to the countryside to work as peasants, that they cannot
do other work. I feel that in the present stage, when a difference still exists between the city and the countryside, between
the worker and the peasant, and between mental labor and manual labor, in a situation where the power of traditional concepts
and habits from the past are still attacking the thoughts of the
people, we should enthusiastically take the lead in sending our
sons and daughters to the villages and participate in the great
socialist revolution of going up to the mountains and down to the
countryside. This is the proper function of a Communist Party
member.

Sending my lower-middle school, upper-middle school, and
college graduate sons and daughters to the countryside to receive reeducation from the poor and lower-middle peasants
corresponds completely with Party policy, and with the teaching
of Chairman Mao that "the successors to the proletarian revolution are born from the struggle of the masses, and grow up
tempered by the great winds and waves of the revolution." Now,
some parents are unwilling to send their sons and daughters to
the countryside, saying that village life is hard and being afraid
their children cannot take it. I feel that this kind of thinking is
incorrect. In the twenty years since liberation, the country's
villages have undergone very great changes. The living standards of the commune members are unceasingly rising. To be
sure, at present, the conditions of life in the villages, compared
with life in the towns, is in fact somewhat harder. But precisely
because it is harder, educated youths should go to be tempered,
give help, unite with poor and lower-middle peasants, and
change the underdevelopment in that area. Everyone should
think about it: if you say your own sons and daughters cannot
tolerate life in the villages, then how can the great masses of
poor and lower-middle peasants who have lived in the villages
for generations tolerate it? We can see that the problem is not
whether or not one can tolerate it, but how to face difficulties
and hardships. We parents must listen to Chairman Mao's
teaching that "the only way to be a good comrade is to go where
the difficulty is greatest" and use it as the principle for sending

our sons and daughters to the countryside. From the change
in my children after they have been to the villages, I find that
they have made the following improvements: First, they have
learned of the poor and lower-middle peasant's love of the
Party, their love for Chairman Mao's profound proletarian
feeling, their distinguishing between love and hate from the
point of view of class, and their fine style of plain living and
hard struggle. They have begun to understand that "every grain
in the bowl is the product of toil" and are acquiring the habits
of industry, economy and love of labor. Gradually they are acquiring the proletarian world view of wholeheartedly serving the
people. I feel that the question of how to deal with the difference
between the towns and the countryside, and the hardships of life,
is related to the great question of whether the young generation
can establish revolutionary thinking, whether they can correctly
recognize the path before them. We who are parents cannot be
shortsighted and only fasten our sights on arranging for "lei-
surely" work for our children, or on setting up a small "comfortable" family world.

Should we keep our sons and daughters by our sides, or should
we let the Party arrange for them? It is a question of principle
whether one will let private notions of "parental love" spoil
sons and daughters, or whether one will use proletarian "class
consciousness" to educate sons and daughters. It importantly
reflects whether or not a cadre has proletarian party spirit.
In our socialist country, sons and daughters are members of
society and belong to the people; they are the wealth of the entire country; we certainly cannot act as though they are the
property of individuals. To carry out the country's socialist
revolution and socialist construction, we must have a unified
plan and a revolutionary division of labor. If, like some cadres,
we only think of keeping our sons and daughters in the towns to
work and are unwilling to send them to the countryside to serve
the peasants, then where would the food that people in towns eat
and the clothes they wear come from? How can we get rid of
the three great differences? How can we realize communism?

Currently the sons and daughters of many workers have declared in ringing words: "Our whole lives are for the Party to
arrange," "Where the Party points, we will go," "We will put
down roots in the border regions to carry out revolution; our
youthful years are offered to the new villages." To be revolutionary cadres, we must study and support this kind of precious
revolutionary fervor of the young people, and teach our sons
and daughters to follow their examples and adhere to the country's unified allocation, instead of picking and choosing for them,
or worse, getting mixed up in some improper arrangement.

Then there are parents who think that for sons and daughters
to go to the villages and work as peasants leaves them without
aspirations and without a future. I feel that under our country's
dictatorship of the proletariat, departure from the great goal
of communism and from the demands of the Party's task for
so-called individual "aspirations," individual "future," can
only be called bourgeois individualism and can never be realized. Many facts prove that after educated youths go to the
countryside they will have lofty aspirations and a great future
if they only accept modestly reeducation from the poor and
lower-middle peasants and are willing to devote their efforts
to building socialism. Han Chih-kang of neighboring Hsing-ping
hsien is a young intellectual who went to the countryside. He
worked with the poor and lower-middle peasants for more than
ten years to make poor and underdeveloped Pei-ma Brigade
into an abundant and flourishing new socialist village and he
was hailed as a "red flag" for the entire province for emulation
of the Tachai agricultural model.* Later Han Chih-kang became the deputy secretary of the Hsing-ping hsien Communist
Party committee and did notable work there. This May he was
selected to be the secretary of the Shensi Communist Youth
League. Recently, the newspapers reported the activities of
Chu Ko-chia, a Shanghai educated youth who went to the countryside, and gave to us yet another model in this vein. Who can

---

*See the Glossary.

say that he is without aspirations? And who can say that he has no future?

The movement of educated youth up to the mountains and down to the countryside is both to cultivate successors to the proletarian revolution and to construct new socialist villages. Hastening the country's agricultural development is a pressing necessity for the economic development of the country; and is a glorious duty that the Party and Chairman Mao have given to the great masses of poor and lower-middle peasants, to cadres in every line of work, and to educated youth. Chairman Mao has taught that "the young people are the most active, most energetic force in the whole society. They are the most willing to learn and the least conservative in thought. This is especially true in the socialist period." It is a fine and generous thing for educated youth to go to the countryside and unite with the masses of poor and lower-middle peasants, to energetically use their two hands in a struggle against the elements, and to construct a new socialist village. We who are parents must maintain the correct direction of sending educated youths up to the mountains and down to the countryside, and we must plant firmly in our minds the thought that "agriculture is the foundation." We must be progressive forces teaching ours sons and daughters to go to the countryside and engage in agriculture. We must do our duty and contribute our share to cultivate and create tens of millions of successors to the proletarian revolution.

13

The Deputy Commander Teaches His
Daughter to Engage in Agriculture*

I

Not long ago a fifty-some-year-old Red Army warrior came
to Chu Village in the northern part of Hai-yang hsien in the old
Anti-Japanese Base Area of Chiao-tung. The keen-eyed commune members knew at a glance that he was Ho Ch'ü-pao, deputy commander of the People's Liberation Army Tsingtao
Military Region, and immediately called: "Aunty Chiang's relative has come!" There was great excitement at Aunty Chiang's
house and commune members were pressing inside and outside
the home. When Ho Yü-t'ang, who was working in the field,
heard that her father had come, she quickly ran home. When
Aunty Chiang saw her daughter-in-law covered with sweat, she
lovingly passed her a handkerchief and cried: "Young lady,
quickly fix your father some food."

Ho Ch'ü-pao was on his way to a meeting and had made a de-
tour to visit his daughter who has settled down here. When
Aunty Chiang saw her relative, her eyes squinted with joy as

_____

*"Fu ssu-ling-yüan chiao nü wu nung."

121

she said to him, "Big brother, a middle-aged woman like me could not imagine even in my dreams having such a daughter-in-law and uniting with such good relatives as you."

Ho Chü-pao said, "Madam, in the old society we were all poor agricultural laborers. In the new society our work posts may be different, but we all serve the people."

Ho Chü-pao asked about Yü-t'ang's situation and the branch secretary, Chou Yü-t'ing, told him: "When this child had just arrived she saw an oxen and was frightened. Now she can till and plow the fields, break down hills and smash stones and do all sorts of things." Aunty Chiang, hearing people praise her daughter-in-law, quickly broke in to join the chorus: "This young lady of mine will plunge right into mud and water!"

Hearing people talk, Ho Chü-pao felt that his daughter had certainly grown up in the big world. She had already changed from a full-grown but childish urban educated youth into a new type of peasant.

II

Nine years earlier, Ho Yü-t'ang was a middle school student in Tsingtao. When she was about to graduate from lower-middle school, she reported for the entrance examination at a military health school, wanting to be a Liberation Army medical worker. She also thought of taking the examination for technical school to prepare to produce machinery for the socialist construction of the motherland. But, on the eve of her graduation the school Party branch wanted to mobilize some of the graduates to go up to the mountains and down to the countryside.

Ho Chü-pao already knew of these matters. For the past several days he had given a great deal of thought to his daughter's work assignment. He thought of when Yü-t'ang was not yet nine and she and her mother lived in Shensi. As soon as she was familiar with the situation she would gather grass with a basket over her arm and graze the sheep; why is it that she is not as diligent and happy now? In the past the millet and cornmeal

bread were both sweet and fragrant. Why is it that today she
will eat a bit and want no more? Considering these changes in
his daughter, he finally decided on a plan. He would send his
daughter to the countryside, let her work to build new socialist
villages, and let her be tempered and grow up in the wide
world. He told this plan to a man who did street work who at
the time was also mobilizing educated youths on the street to
go up to the mountains and down to the countryside. He thought
the man's plan was correct and said that cadres should lead the way.

One day after school Ho Ch'ü-pao called his daughter to his
side and asked her: "Yü-t'ang, what will you do after graduation?" She innocently replied, "What do you think, Papa?" Ho
Ch'ü-pao told her that he was preparing to send her to the
countryside. As soon as Yü-t'ang heard that she broke into
laughter saying, "Papa, I have already signed up!" As she
talked she placed in front of her papa the paper indicating assignment preference after graduation. He saw only the fourteen
characters written at the very top: "Those who have answered
the Party's call to settle down in the rural villages."

Father and daughter thought alike. Ho Ch'ü-pao said to Yü-
t'ang with emotion: "Our ancestors were farmers. It is only in
your generation that we moved to the city. Times have changed
and the significance is very different when you respond to the
Party's call as you have today and want to become a farmer."
He wanted his daughter to learn from her mother, and said,
"When we were in northern Shensi and participating in the
'worker, peasant, Red Army to the front line' movement, your
mother and other villagers who were at home organized labor
exchange teams and mutual-aid organizations to vigorously engage in all sorts of activities like plowing the fields and chop-
ping firewood. You should fervently love the agricultural villages and labor like your mother." The father's words gave the
daughter new strength and urged her in a new direction.

III

Full of warm feelings, the poor and lower-middle peasants
of Chu Village received Ho Yü-t'ang and her classmates. Earlier

they had discussed and agreed that they wanted these youths who had just left their fathers and mothers to be as happy in their living situation as if they were in their own homes.

The day after Ho Yü-t'ang and her classmates arrived was the Mid-Autumn Festival. The poor and lower-middle peasants of Chu Village, fearing that they would be homesick, urged them into their own homes to celebrate. The commune members sent them taro, rue beans, and melons and even sent them little bundles of wheat stalks to sit on while eating. Aunty Chou, who is over seventy years old, leaned on her cane and made pao-tzu [steamed bread with a filling] especially for them and personally brought them over. In the evening many people came over to where Yü-t'ang and the others were staying. The three-room dwelling was filled with people. Yü-t'ang was very happy to spend the very first holiday in the village with so many people. She was so excited she did not sleep half the night.

But a battle test that would transform the heavens and change the earth presently awaited her. Not long after Yü-t'ang came to the village she and others went up the mountain to hoe field melons. The five-foot hoe felt like a one hundred chin iron baton in her hand. On the first day, the others hoed over one mou, but although she had rubbed five big blood blisters on her hands, she had hoed only a half to two-thirds as much. When she went to the field on the second day the grass was still growing as before! Yü-t'ang scrutinizing her blood blisters thought, "This is just the beginning. Will I be able to continue as the days pass?"

Several months later, Ho Ch'ü-pao came to Chu Village for the first time. Ever since Yü-t'ang had left his side, he had thought constantly about her training situation in the village, and because he was somewhat worried he decided to go and see for himself.

When Yü-t'ang saw her father she was extremely happy. This child who always liked to talk and laugh talked more than ever that day. She talked about how an aunty in the eastern part of the village had taught her how to make clothes and how a gentleman in the west had taught her farming. When she talked about how she had gotten blood blisters, Ho Ch'ü-pao chuckled,

"That's nothing. When you get a few calluses you won't get any
more blisters."

Yü-t'ang was encouraged by her father's words. That evening she searched out the production team leader and said,
"From now on give me the team's heavy and tiring work to do."

After her papa left, Yü-t'ang acquired new strength. In the
daytime she labored in the fields, and in the evening she ran a
night school in the village to help the poor and lower-middle
peasants study culture. When winter came she strove to be first
among the able-bodied laborers to gather stones in the mountains to repair the drains, and to do hammering and welding and
other such work. Year after year she lived, worked, and transformed her thinking together with the poor and lower-middle
peasants. She learned many things that cannot be learned in
cities and schools. She understood the hardships encountered
by her revolutionary forebears. She understood how she should
struggle hard and temper herself to become a successor to the
proletarian revolutionary cause.

IV

When she had grown older, Ho Yü-t'ang encountered a new
problem on the road ahead: how would she handle the questions
of love, marriage, and a home? There was a youth named
Chiang P'ing. This lad's father died young, and when he was
seven years old, before liberation, he and his mother begged
for food. When he was twelve he went to labor on the land.
Chiang P'ing, who grew up immersed in bitter water, loved the
village and loved labor. He was a good hand on the farm production line. After Yü-t'ang arrived here, Chiang P'ing fervently
taught her to cultivate the fields, and she patiently taught him
to study culture. The two of them had rather deep feelings for
each other.

But, for a youth so inclined to love, Yü-t'ang's heart was not
without inner struggle. She felt that this youth was worthy of
her love, but she also thought that loving him meant making a
decision to spend the rest of her life in the village. While having

this struggle with her thoughts, she studied again Chairman Mao's teaching that "whoever among the intellectuals can go to the villages to work should gladly go. The villages are a vast universe where one can be of great use." Chairman Mao's teaching elevated Yü-t'ang's thinking to a new level. She thought, "I have come here to construct new socialist villages and not to get a patina of experience. Since Chiang P'ing loves the village and loves labor so much, why can't I live here for a lifetime with him?" In this way Yü-t'ang's love for Chiang P'ing was decided.

When the news of this situation circulated, some people were inclined not to believe it. They said: "Yü-t'ang is a cultured person and Chiang P'ing has not gone to school. How can this be?"

When Yü-t'ang told her parents of her marriage plans, her mother felt at the time that since she herself was getting old, and was frequently ill, she wished that Yü-t'ang could find a partner in a nearby area, and that they could look after each other. Ho Ch'ü-pao listened to his wife's thinking and felt that he agreed; but when he thought it over in detail, he felt it was incorrect. Since his daughter was in the village to settle down, why should she not find a partner there? He upheld Yü-tang's choice.

After Yü-t'ang was married, Ho Ch'ü-pao again told his daughter that she must not feel too ecstatic, but must actively participate in collective labor and follow her mother in establishing a new-style home.

As of today this pair of young companions, united in labor and struggle, are advancing shoulder to shoulder. Because Chiang P'ing's cultural level was low, Yü-t'ang helped him in his cultural studies. Chiang P'ing became the brigade Party branch secretary. Yü-t'ang voluntarily did more of the housework to enable him to devote more energy to his work. As for Chiang P'ing, he also voluntarily shared in the housework to enable Yü-t'ang to spend more time participating in collective production and social activities. The commune members, seeing the young husband and wife united this way in love and mutual respect, honored them for being correct and good and praised them for changing styles and customs and for taking the lead in introducing new trends.

V

In the beginning of 1971, Ho Yü-t'ang, who had lived and struggled in Chu Village for seven winters and springs, saw a number of the educated youths who had come to Chu Village with her to settle suddenly leave to take new work positions. She began to wonder: "What will I do now that they have gone?" Someone who had noticed her concern said, "Can't you talk to your papa and return?" Yü-t'ang thought "That won't do. Papa's power is given to him by the people. He must use it to plan the welfare of the broad masses. I cannot request that papa do this kind of thing."

Once when she was visiting her home, Yü-t'ang reported this problem to her father. Ho Ch'ü-pao felt that his daughter had done the right thing, but he discerned that his daughter's determination to settle in the village was wavering. He didn't answer his daughter's question directly, but asked: "Is your area completely transformed? Is the construction of your brigade completed?" Yü-t'ang knew from her father's string of rhetorical questions that her thinking was incorrect. Seeing that his daughter understood, he continued by saying, "This kind of wavering clearly indicates that you must continue to be tempered."

Carrying new thoughts with her, Yü-t'ang flew back to Chu Village. The day after she arrived at her home she felt disquieted. She went to the areas where she had struggled shoulder to shoulder with the poor and lower-middle peasants and inspected the mountains here and the waters there. When she came to the forest temple and the mountain foothills, layer upon layer of tidy, terraced fields dazzled her eyes. A few years ago this area had been all ditches and gullies; now well-regulated and irrigated fields were everywhere. In the past, the production per mou did not exceed 300 chin at most. Now it had already reached over 570 chin. In those years they had to rely on two oxen and one plow. Now over 40 percent of the land of the entire brigade is machine cultivated. On a misty knoll she looked over the 100 mou apple orchard and clearly remembered a recent year when they had gathered only four apples. This year they had gathered over 30,000 chin. At Cinnamon Tree Mountain reservoir, Yü-t'ang looked at the irrigation ditch that she herself had helped to build. It was already connected and spouting, irrigating over 300 mou of arable fields.

Yü-t'ang looked and thought as she walked. She asked herself questions and answered them: "Have the changes been great in Chu Village? The changes have truly been great, guided by Chairman Mao's revolutionary line and learning from Tachai in agriculture. Is it finished? No. This is only the beginning. For instance, although one can say that we have crossed the "Yellow River" in grain production, there is still much land that is not as orderly as the terraced fields at Tachai; and although the trees have become a woods and fruit fills the branches, there are still 800 or 900 mou of wild mountain land in the brigade that has not been planted with trees; and although water conservancy is much better than in the past, on three-quarters of the land free-flowing irrigation is not yet possible. The fields must continue to be put in order, trees must continue to be planted, water must continue to be found and the town itself must continue to be constructed. That my fellow students have gone to the industrial battle line and I have remained on the agricultural battle line — both are necessary for revolution. Yü-t'ang's thinking was greatly expanded when she reached this point. She squeezed hard the rock that was in her hand, and said with determination "I won't leave this place. This is my battleground."

Two years have passed since then. Yü-t'ang has not forsaken the cultivation of her Party, the education of her family, or the expectations of the poor and lower-middle peasants. By her own activities, she has put her words into practice. Regardless of the season, even when she awakes in the bitter cold, she never misses work without a reason. She eats revolutionary bitterness and does strenuous work. People praise her as an unashamed daughter of a Red Army warrior and a descendant of the revolution.

Appendix

A Thought-Provoking Test Answer Sheet *

"People's Daily" Editor's Note

Under the title "A Thought-Provoking Test Answer Sheet," the Liao-ning jih-pao of July 19 carried a letter from a rusticated educated youth along with an editor's note. This letter posed an important problem in the struggle between the two lines and the two kinds of ideology on the educational front. It is really thought-provoking.

It has been five years since the publication of Chairman Mao's directive, "It is imperative to select students from among workers and peasants with practical experience. After a few years' study in school they must return to production." The struggle-criticism-transformation campaign on the educational front is deepening. We must seriously study and resolutely carry out Chairman Mao's directive, make investigations and studies, sum up experiences, and do a good job in the proletarian educational revolution.

*   *   *

---

*Jen-min jih-pao [People's Daily], August 10, 1973. This translation is taken from Survey of China Mainland Press, No. 73 (August 20-24, 1973), 112-114.

"Liao-ning Daily" Editor's Note

Printed here is a letter written by Comrade Chang T'ieh-sheng on the back of a test sheet related to the enrollment of university students this year.

Comrade Chang T'ieh-sheng is a young intellectual and Communist Youth League member who came to the countryside in 1968. He is now the leader of No. 4 Production Team of Tsao-shan Brigade, Pai-t'a Commune. He seemed to have turned in a "blank" in the examination for physics and chemistry. Yet as far as the question of the line in the enrollment of university students as a whole is concerned, he did submit an answer that was meaningful and thought-provoking.

To select and send to universities outstanding workers, peasants, and rusticated educated youths with practical experience in accordance with Chairman Mao's proletarian educational line is a major reform in our educational system. It is warmly hailed by the broad masses. Meanwhile, resistance will immediately come from various old ideas and the force of old habits. In the enrollment of university students, a proper cultural examination on the basis of mass assessment and mass recommendation is necessary. But is the purpose of a cultural examination mainly for finding out the ability to analyze and solve problems or for checking how many middle school lessons are still borne in mind? Is the main criterion for admission based on one's consistent performance in the Three Great Revolutionary Movements or the marks in a cultural examination? Is it an encouragement for educated youths to receive reeducation from the poor and lower-middle peasants and the working class and to strive to delve into and fulfill their own work tasks, or an encouragement for them to depart from the practice of the Three Great Revolutionary Movements to study behind closed doors? The purpose of our publishing Comrade Chang T'ieh-sheng's letter today is to in-

vite a discussion and study of these problems by everyone, and we welcome opinions from those comrades concerned with the educational revolution.

* * *

Respected leaders:
The written examination is over for me. In this respect, I
have some feelings which I would like to discuss with the
leadership.

Since I came to the countryside in 1968, I have at all times
devoted myself heart and soul to agricultural production and
given my all to the duties of my post. Around eighteen hours
of heavy manual labor and work per day did not allow me time
for a review of my vocational studies. What time I had was only
after the receipt of the notice on the twenty-seventh. During the
examination period, I hurriedly glanced through the mathematics teaching material. Concerning questions of geometry and
those about physics and chemistry presented in today's test
paper, I could only stare at them helplessly. I am not willing
to answer the questions at random without basing myself on
books; this would just waste the time of the leadership in reading my paper. So I would rather observe discipline, stick it out,
and pull out honestly. Frankly speaking, I just can't reconcile
myself to those bookworms who have for years just loafed about
without any regular employment. I have a strong feeling against
them. The examination is being cornered by this group of college fans. At the height of summer-hoeing and production, I
just couldn't bear to drop production work and shut myself in a
small house. This would be too selfish. Should I do that, I
would have felt a prick of conscience owing to my sense of responsibility toward the revolutionary cause for myself and the
poor and lower-middle peasants, and toward making revolution
against self. One source of comfort to me is that I have let
nothing interfere with collective work. In the production team,
I have discharged my full and complete responsibilities. When
the welcomed spring rain came, people really had their hands

full. Under this situation of a direct clash between the interests of the individual and the collective, (it may be said that) this was quite a struggle. What saddens me is that a few hours of written tests could mean the loss of my qualifications for admission. I will not talk about anything else. But I will always feel there is really something that I cannot get off my chest. My ideals from childhood are being chased away and superseded by my own work. This is the only justification I have to stress.

I have attended the study class in compliance with the new enrollment system and requirements. As to my fundamental knowledge, since the examination site is my alma mater, the teachers here should know and remember that it is not bad at all. Though the questions of physics and chemistry raised in the examination sheet today are very shallow, my own understanding is equally shallow. With two days' time allowed to review my lessons, I can guarantee giving answers to score full marks.

I have a clean record as far as my own political outlook, my family background and my relations with society are concerned. For a city-bred child like me, it has been really very exacting training in the past few years. Especially when it comes to ideological feelings and the transformation of the world outlook, I may claim a leap in my progress. Here I have not filled out the test sheet in conformity with the set requirements and the system (which renders impossible an assessment of my background knowledge and ability); I don't feel ashamed of that. I may as well try to make it. By just referring to books, I could also get several dozen marks (which is meaningless)! But I don't feel very happy at heart about doing that. What I take pride in is that only under the new educational system and through the willing recommendation of the poor and lower-middle peasants and the leading cadres could I have attended this study class.

Examinee Chang T'ieh-sheng
of the Pai-t'a Commune

June 30, 1973

Report on an Application to Leave the University

Chung Chih-min*

"People's Daily" Editor's Note

This report on an application to leave school by Chung Chih-min, a student in the political science department of Nanking University, is a voluntary criticism of his error of entering the university through the "back door." It reflects the development of a new attack on landlord and bourgeois consciousness by the worker, peasant, and soldier students. It also reflects the angry revolutionary atmosphere of the educational battle line.

This report brings up two important questions: (1) Are the sons and daughters of revolutionary cadres to grow up tempered by the winds and waves of the Three Great Revolutionary Movements? Or are they to rest on their parents' "merit books" and enjoy "special treatment"? (2) Are the revolutionary cadres teaching their sons and daughters to take the road of uniting with workers and peasants and become successors of proletarian revolutionary cause? Or are they regarding their sons and daughters as "private property" and "using the back

---

*Chung Chih-min, "I-fen t'ui-hsüeh shen-ch'ing pao-kao." Jen-min jih-pao [People's Daily], January 18, 1974.

135

door" of the university as a ladder to success? We suggest that everyone read the essay "Ch'u Che admonishes
the Chao Empress Dowager" in Intrigues of the Warring
States [Chan-kuo ts'e] and take a look at the story of
how Ch'u Che admonishes the Chao Empress Dowager to
not coddle her own little son Chang An-chun! It is an inside story of the exploiting class. We do not represent
the exploiting class. We represent the proletariat and
the working people. But if we are not careful to make
strict demands on our sons and daughters, they can also
degenerate and restore the regime of the bourgeoisie.
The property and power of the proletariat can then be
snatched back by the bourgeoisie. This is truly an important question relating to opposing and guarding
against revisionism, and to nuturing tens of millions of
successors to the proletarian revolutionary cause. Is it
not worth our serious attention?

*   *   *

Dear Party Committee of the University:
I am a student from the army who "used the back door" to enter the university. Last year when the universities were taking
applications from students, under the influence of my repeated
pleadings, my father telephoned the cadre section of the military
district asking them to appoint me and send me to the university.
I have studied at the university for more than a year, particularly under the admonition that "the humanities must use the
entire society as their factory." When I went to mines and factories and came into contact with some workers and masses
and with some social problems, I began to realize that many of
my past ways of thinking were incorrect and gradually recognized that "using the back door" is not a small matter of no significance, but is related to the important matter of which course
to take. Because it pertains to a matter of such a fundamental
nature, it is a question of the meaning of being a person, of
whether to use the authority that the people have delegated to
serve the people, or whether to use it to serve one's private

ends! Chairman Mao says, "All of us working cadres, regardless of rank, are servants of the people; everything we do is to
serve the people." However, using methods like going through
the "back door" takes advantage of the authority given by the
people for one's own private gain; it is not acting according to
the principles of the Party, but is going counter to the principles
of the Party. To get their sons and daughters into the university, some parents do not go through the process of recommendation and selection by the masses, do not go through the legiti-
mating procedure of the Party organization, but rely on their
official authority and power and on personal feelings and relationships to solve problems. Some people even use university
admissions as "gifts," giving them here and there, pushing and
pulling, and actually shutting the outstanding representatives
of the real workers, peasants, and soldiers outside the university gates. Can this kind of action be serving the people? No.
This is something from the bourgeoisie. This kind of improper
practice is like a plague, eroding our Party, destroying the relationship between the Party and the people, and harming the
great tradition of the Party, it is completely at odds with the
nature of a proletarian party.

To "establish a party for all" or to "establish a party for
self," that is the touchstone that distinguishes all true and false
Party members. Why is it that some are always thinking about
sending their own sons and daughters to the university, and do
not think to follow the Party's principles and send the outstanding representatives of the workers, peasants, and soldiers to
the university? It is simply because they feel that these are
their own children, and those are other people's children, so
before doing anything, they calculate their own self-interest.
Why is it that some people are always thinking of sending their
sons and daughters to the university, and not of letting them go
to the villages, the factories, and the army? It is simply because they think that the new socialist universities are like
those before, and are the steps to fame and family fortune,
that going to university will result in "advancement and knowledge."

The ideological basis of "using the back door" is the residual bourgeois concept of private ownership. The social basis of "using the back door" is the residual bourgeois judicial power. In a word, "using the back door" is not proletarian, it is bourgeois. The reckless plot to restore capitalism by Lin Piao and the bourgeois clique within the Party used improper "back door" methods like boasting and flattery, pulling and dragging to win over and corrupt our cadres, to form cliques for selfish ends, and to divide and destroy our Party. If we want to practice Marxism-Leninism, to unite, and to be open and honest, we must vigorously fight against such improper methods as "using the back door." If we do not topple this type of wrongdoing, then the proletarian revolution cannot be carried out to its utmost socialism. This is a question of time.

The authority given by the people is meant to be used only to serve the people; certainly it cannot be used to plot for one's own selfish interests or those of a few people. Because we are the Communist Party, and not the Kuomintang, we use political power to serve the people and not to oppress the people. When the first people's government, the Paris Commune, was born, Marx pointed out: "Every privilege and every allowance that the high officials of the country enjoyed were wiped out with the wiping out of these high officials. The offices of society are no longer the private property of the errand boys of the central government." During the Proletarian Cultural Revolution, our great Chairman Mao with even greater clarity pointed out: "The most basic condition for the reform of government agencies is to unite with the masses." Only by following these principles can we guarantee that our country will not change color, can we guarantee that our cadres will not become revisionists, can we thoroughly carry forward our socialist revolution!

A, cadre of the Party should work hard to serve the people, and not play at "being special." The children of cadres have even less right to become separated from the masses and become bourgeois "young mistresses and young masters."

In the past I have always felt that my family background is

good. My father from the time of Ching-kang-shan* has followed
Chairman Mao in making revolution; he took part in the Long
March, and took part in the war against Japan; from the time of
resisting the Americans and aiding the Koreans to the front lines
at Tunghai.... Born in a family with such "contributions" to the
revolution, and recipient of such special attention, is there anything that is out of bounds?

No, this type of thinking is wrong! Why is it that the children
of cadres cannot leave the "special care" of their fathers and
mothers to go and build their own lives? What have we done for
the people? What right have we to enjoy being looked after?
To enter a university on the strength of a telephone call is not
right. The thinking of the people who think that they are born
into good families as though they are better than others in character and deserve to enjoy "being special" is especially dangerous. If it is allowed to develop, they could very easily move
toward being a "privileged stratum"; they could very easily become revisionist.

Our great revolutionary teacher Chairman Mao has in many
writings repeatedly stressed the possibility of this kind of
change and degeneration. The appearance of Soviet social im-
perialism and the activities of the Proletarian Cultural Revolution have enabled us to see even more clearly this point: if
the children of cadres who have lived for long periods of time
in a relatively comfortable environment, and who have been
separated for long periods of time from the masses of workers
and peasants, and from productive labor, do not attend to transforming their own world view, they will relatively easily by
captured by the ideology of the bourgeoisie, and they will relatively easily become revisionist. What I am saying, naturally,
includes myself and began as words to myself.

How dangerous it is that revisionism should appear in us!
Father, Mother, will the hard road through the mountains and
rivers beaten out with the blood of our revolutionary forebears
be lost for good before us? No, definitely not! We should not

---

*See the Glossary.

rely on our fathers and mothers for our livelihood. Politically, we must succeed to their mission and carry to the end the proletarian revolution which they have not completed.

To be true soldiers of the proletarian revolution we must decide to thoroughly reform ourselves. The "back door" and other such actions are not beneficial to the reform of our world view; they help us escape from the fire of struggle; they lead us to take the path of individualism; they definitely are a "ghost gate" which befuddles people and leads toward capitalism.

Dear Party committee of the university, the above is my understanding of my "using the back door" to enter the university. These thoughts gradually took shape before the summer vacation, and during the vacation I discussed my thinking with my father and mother; they both supported my thinking; both agreed with my understanding of this question. After I returned to the university, I discussed this again with comrades in the department. Now, having studied the documents of the [October 1973] Tenth Party Congress, I have strengthened even more my resolution to correct my errors. Chairman Mao says, "Our duty is to serve the people. Every sentence, every action, every policy, must be for the people's benefit. If there is an error, we must correct it; this is called carrying out responsibility toward the people." I was not recommended; nor was I selected; and most important, I did not enter the university according to the principles of the Party and the procedures of student admission. Therefore, I apply to the Party Committee of the university to allow me to return to the military.

I am determined to return to the military to accept humbly reeducation from the workers, peasants, and soldiers, to work hard to reconstruct my nonproletarian thinking, to temper myself in the Three Great Revolutionary Movements, and to be a true successor to the proletarian revolutionary cause.

Obediently,

I salute you in the revolution!

Department of Political Science
Philosophy Major Chung Chih-min
September 28, 1973

The Older Generation Fought to Make Revolution, We Must Also Make Revolution

Comrade Chung Chih-min Discusses the Thinking behind His Application to Withdraw from the University*

(Jen-min jih-pao) On the morning of January 17, the entire standing committee of the Party Committee of Nanking University met and listened to a briefing by Comrade Chung Chih-min, a second year student in the department of political science, regarding his thoughts on the question of applying to withdraw from the university. The report is printed below.

The Party committee has been very concerned about the matter of my application to withdraw from the university. Originally, my thoughts were crafty and I did not feel honorable. Now I understand that the revolutionary road of Chairman Mao is incomparably correct, and the leadership of the Party is incomparably warm.

I entered the university by "using the back door." This was an error. I graduated from lower middle school in 1968 and went to work in a brigade of Sha-chou-pa Commune in Jui-chin hsien. At first I did not want to go. As things developed, my

---

*Chung Chih-min t'ung-chih t'an shen-ch'ing t'ui-hsüeh ti ssu-hsiang ching-kuo. "Lao-pei ta-chang kan ko-ming, wo-men yeh yao ko-ming." Jen-min jih-pao [People's Daily], January 29, 1974.

141

parents told me, "Go first and later we will have you transferred back." In 1969, when the military was recruiting, I went to the military department to look for political committee member Tu, and he accepted me right away. I joined the army by using the military slot of another commune. In that commune, a commune member had already passed his physical, and could enter the army at once. However, his slot was given to me, and that commune member could not go. At Sha-chou-pa Commune I had only forty to fifty work points. After I entered the military, I wanted very much to go to the university to learn something. I had spoken of it to my parents many times, feeling that it was only natural for the children of cadres to get special attention. In April 1972, when the universities were accepting applicants, my father was in charge of work for cadres in the military district. He telephoned the departments concerned, and it was very quickly arranged that I could go to the university. Before I entered the university, my mother called me again and asked me what I wanted to study. I said I would like to study philosophy, and thus I entered the university. Before I left, some of the cadres and comrades of the Fuchow military district talked to me about my going, and when I left, I felt a bit ashamed. After I arrived at the university, I wanted very much to write to the unit; I wanted to write that "never will I betray the trust of the Party organization," but knowing that I was not here by the election of the organization, I never had the courage to write. After I came to the university, I learned a few things and, in addition, came into contact with some workers and peasants; I went to the Nanking auto factory and the Feng-huang-shan Iron Mine, and the People's Market, and heard the dissatisfaction of many people with the practice of "using the back door." Thinking of my own case, I felt that "using the back door" to go to the university was not right. I was especially concerned last year, about May or June, when I went to the Feng-huang-shan Iron Mine to carry out open-door schooling there, and heard the great "Letter of Chairman Mao to Comrade Li Chung-lin" and the extremely strong responses of the worker masses; these are things that I could not have heard in school. My thoughts were greatly disturbed, and I felt that I had done wrong. I should be struggling, and oppose these types of things. That summer when I returned home, I spoke of these things to my mother, and she was very moved and recognized that matters had not been handled correctly. But she disagreed that I should leave and return to the military. She said it would be a bad influence and that the children of some leading cadres have not left either. My sister's husband said that I was guilty of extreme "leftism," that I felt that "only I can carry out the revolution." We discussed this problem every day during the summer vacation. My mother repeatedly said that it was enough if you recognize your error, that it was not necessary to leave the university, and she wanted me to discuss it thoroughly before deciding. My father was very busy with his work, and I talked with him only once. At first my father also felt that it was not necessary to leave. I pointed out to him that it is not right that the children of leading cadres do not go to the villages, as if Marxism-Leninism were only for others. At last he expressed the view that "a peasant in the family is good, too." The other members of the family also did not agree with my action. When I returned to the university, I sought out a teacher and explained that I had "used the back door" to enter the university. At the same time, I wrote again to the family, asking to leave the university. The family, in its reply, did not agree with my leaving; my mother said, you are a Party member, you can write a briefing on your thoughts to the Party organization, and if the organization decides that you should leave, then you should leave; if it does not decide that you should leave, then you should go on with your lessons. Later on, after studying the documents of the Tenth Party Congress, I did write a report and waited to hear the decision of the Party committee as to whether I should leave. At that time, I was still not clear about whether or not I should leave. A relative of mine said that leaving school can be seen in a specific situation as a leftist act disturbing the revolutionary line of Chairman Mao. In the country, there are so many people "using the back door"; if you act this way, you will indeed create a mess. I remember that Chairman Wang (Chairman Wang Yung of the Nanking Uni-

versity Revolutionary Committee) had made three points to me
when we talked: (1) Since your problem arose before the pro-
mulgation of the 1972 Central Committee Document No. 19, and
that document does not cover leaving the university, you do not
need to leave; (2) your fellow students and your teachers have
reacted well to you, there is no necessity to leave the university; (3) to leave after studying for a year and a half is a loss to
the country as well. After that, I considered thoroughly the
question of whether or not I ought to leave, feeling as though the
matter had not come to an end. At that time I went to Fu-ning
hsien to participate in the rectification of the standing committee
of the hsien committee, and finding that the masses had a great
many opinions concerning the committee members, I thought of
myself and my family and realized that my problem was not an
individual problem but a problem of struggling against improper
influences within the Party, a problem of which road to take.
Thus I determined that I must return. After my return, my
thinking was greatly shaken, and I deeply felt the warmth of the
correct path of the Party. Since I was taking this course of
action, and the path was correct, I ought to carry it out to the
end, return to the army, and go to a farming village.

On this question, how should we view the children of cadres?
Thinking back, I remember that at the beginning of the Cultural
Revolution, while I was a Red Guard at the Nan-chang No. 2 Middle School, I thought that the reactionary "theory of blood relationships" was correct, that "if the father is a hero, the son
is a stalwart fellow"; "if the father is a reactionary, the son is
a bastard." I had even written big-character posters supporting
the "theory of blood relationships." However, thinking on this
question now, I feel a bit concerned; exactly how much revolutionary feeling is there in the children of some cadres? How
many children of cadres are capable of becoming Marxist-
Leninists? The children of cadres enjoy a lot of special privileges. I have a cousin who, when she returns home for vacation, wants the family to send a car to meet her, feeling that
it is shameful to take the bus. Once, when the family car did
not meet her, she got a ride in the car of the military district

office, but did not go home; first she went to the guest house, and then called home to have the car sent out to meet her. I have said that she is guilty of special privileges and has removed herself from the masses. If the children of high-ranking cadres want to become Marxist-Leninists, they must change themselves thoroughly and reconstruct their thinking.

Such practices as "using the back door" do great harm to the Party and must be fought against. If you do not fight against them, then you are speaking empty words. Before, I felt that the question of "using the back door" was a minor matter; then, after going to Fu-ning hsien to work, I saw the grave nature of the problem of opening the back door. The Party, in order to carry out Marxism-Leninism, must defeat the practice of "using the back door." This relates to the question of acting for oneself or acting for the common people.

I began to have a great many thoughts about going to the villages and putting roots down there for life. Life in the villages is bitter. If I put down roots for a lifetime and my parents should die what would happen? The question of individualism was still not resolved.

In order to resolve my thinking about settling in a village, I returned last year during the summer vacation to Jui-chin. I bought a carton of cigarettes and a few pounds of candy and thought to return for a visit to the place where I had originally joined the work brigade. Reaching the edge of the village, I felt ashamed of going in. What was I? Was I in the army? Was I a university student? Everyone there has to work for five or six years; I was there for three months only and then left. I felt ashamed to go back. Therefore I turned around and went to my uncle's home in Yeh-p'ing Commune and lived there for three days. Some of my cousins and I talked about past events in the family, and I learned a great deal. My grandfather was killed by the enemy. In the winter of 1928, Comrade Yang Tse-kuang of the Red Army came from Min-nan to Jui-chin and lived at my family's, using the position of tutor as a cover for doing underground work. My grandfather was his communications officer and helped him carry out a great deal of work. Under his tutelage, my grandfather gradually learned much revolutionary knowledge. In the winter of 1929, they went to the Kuangsha region to organize disruption activities and formed the fifth regiment of the Workers and Peasants Red Army Crimson Guards Brigade, and my grandfather became chairman of the village soviet. At that time Jui-chin was a guerrilla area, and after the Red Army left, the landlords and local militia returned, and the village people all scattered into the mountains. In the village there was a soldier's dependent who, because of illness, did not leave. My grandfather came down from the mountain to carry him back, but was captured on the road, taken into the temple, and cruelly beaten to force him to reveal the whereabouts of the Red Army and the whereabouts of the villagers. My grandfather would not talk, so the enemy shot him twice; my grandfather did not die, but continued to berate them without ceasing; then the enemy used a knife to kill him, and he was thus martyred. At that time, the family was very poor and could not even afford to buy a coffin, so, using a length of cloth to bind up his wounded stomach, they buried him. After liberation, when removing him to a grave, a bullet was removed from his ribs. My grandmother decided then to send her three sons into the army. My father was only fourteen years old when the three brothers entered the Red Army. Later, my oldest uncle, because one of his legs had been broken by an enemy shell, did not participate in the Long March. Recovering from his wound at home, he was killed by a landlord. My father and second older uncle participated in the Long March. During the Long March, my uncle was wounded, one of his arms being blown off by enemy fire. My father reached Yenan before he knew that my uncle died while crossing the grassy plains.

Thinking of my own life, I feel that I am not worthy of the older revolutionary generation. We are now enjoying the fruits of a revolution that our fathers and mothers won with their blood. We lie sleeping on the merit books of the older generation. When I went to the university, I lost a watch worth more than 400 yuan, but thought nothing of it; later my family bought another one worth more than 180 yuan. In matters of livelihood we have big feet and hands and yet we do not strive to go forward politically. Going on in this way, we may become the betrayers of the revolutionaries of the older generation! Can the socialist land that our revolutionary forebears won with their blood and sacrifices be lost in the hands of our generation? No, it cannot! The older generation fought to make revolution; we too must now make revolution!

I was born in 1952, and before I was a month old, my father went to support the Koreans; since my mother's regiment was also preparing to go to Korea, I was placed at the home of an old woman near the encampment, and only later was I brought back. I was brought up among the masses of the people, and I ought to do my utmost to serve the people. When I participated in the rectification movement of Fu-ning hsien, I saw that in the thirty plus years since liberation, there has been great progress, but there are also many backward and reactionary things. Having learned that socialist revolution is a long and difficult process, I am grieved to think of my errors. The question of who wins and who loses in the Chinese revolution has not really been resolved; there still remains the danger of a revival of capitalism.

There is still a struggle over guidelines in the Party. In the world now, there are many socialist countries which have become revisionist. The proletariat of the whole world is looking to us. Yet with some people, Marxism-Leninism has become a cosmetic. They talk about Marxism-Leninism with their mouths, but in reality they do not do things in a Marxist-Leninist way. If we want to support and consolidate the dictatorship of the proletariat and thoroughly carry out the proletarian revolution, we must steadfastly implement Chairman Mao's revolutionary line, and together with the masses of revolutionary cadres and the masses of workers, peasants, and soldiers fight to the end against the counterrevolutionary revisionism of Lin Piao and fight to the end against the antiproletarian thoughts in our ranks and in our heads. This is for the basic good of the people of China and the people of the world.

I hope that the Party committee will support my action. When I return, I will perform my duties properly.

A Very Good Model

An Investigative Report on the Factory-Commune Links
of the Town of Chu-chou, and the Collective Settlement
of Educated Youths in Commune and Brigade Farms,
Forest Areas, and Tea Plantations*

The town of Chu-chou in Hunan Province, carrying out the
great directive of Chairman Mao that "educated youths must
go to the villages," has put into practice factory-commune
links, and under the leadership of cadres, has made a collective
settlement of educated youths in commune and brigade farms,
forest areas, and tea plantations. In the last two years the entire town has located more than 8,000 educated youths using
this method of settlement. This is a valuable undertaking by
the people of Chu-chou, and it is enthusiastically hailed by
workers, peasants, and educated youths.

<u>Comprehensive Planning</u>   <u>Factory-Commune Links</u>

Chu-chou is a newly developed industrial town, and every factory in Chu-chou <u>hsien</u> and in the area surrounding the town has

---

*Chu-chou shih ch'ang-she kua-kou, chi-t'i an-chih chih-shih
ch'ing-nien tao she-tui nung, lin, ch'a-ch'ang ti tiao-ch'a pao-
kao. "I-ko heng-hao ti tien-hsing." <u>Jen-min jih-pao</u> [People's
Daily], June 12, 1974.

148

its own agricultural support station. Following the development
of industry, factory-managed schools have also been opened.
They make up more than 50 percent of the schools in the entire
town. In 1971, some of the factories collectively delegated the
students who had graduated from these factory-managed schools
to the agricultural support stations.

Chu-chou hsien and the area surrounding the town of Chu-chou
is hilly, "seven parts mountain, one part water, and two parts
field." There are more than 200,000 mou of mountain land, the
greater part of which has not been cultivated in the past. During
the Great Proletarian Cultural Revolution, the mass movement
to learn from Tachai in agriculture in the hsien and the town's
surrounding areas reached a high tide, and year after year rich
crops were harvested. Every commune team unceasingly attacked the depth and breadth of production, attacked the mountain areas, and opened up more than 400 farms, forest areas,
and tea plantations. They urgently needed large numbers of
educated youths from the cities and towns to settle there and
work.

The great rectification movement to criticize Lin Piao raised
the consciousness of the Chu-chou committee toward ideological
line struggle; it recognized that sending educated youth up to the
mountains and down to the countryside is a great socialist revolution. It is a great task for the entire Party, and the people of
the entire country, which requires thoroughly arousing the revolutionary enthusiasm of the people in the city and the countryside who must work in concert to achieve this end. The town
committee began planning on the basis of actual conditions and
needs of the people of the town and countryside. It summarized
the experiences of the masses and proposed the method of factory-commune links and of collectively settling educated youths
in the commune team farms, forest areas, and tea plantations.
The town committee worked out a comprehensive plan for each
factory, office, etc., and the rural commune team to form
bonds with each other based on the conditions and needs of the
villages for taming the mountains and creating forests, on the
size of the factory, and on the number of graduating students.

Large factories formed links with one or several communes;
small factories formed bonds with one commune or one brigade;
agencies in Party and government offices, cultural, educational,
health, financial and trade units systematically formed links
with communes. In addition, large factories provided guidance
for small factories and for organizations. The educated youths
are settled in the agricultural support stations attached to the
factories. Before the educated youths go to the countryside, the
factories send someone to the place where they are settling to
make a report to the commune Party committee and the brigade
Party branch on the educated youths and the situations of their
parents, and together they consider the problems of location,
assignment to groups, and construction of houses.

At present, the entire town already has more than 300 middle
school graduates working in units in factories, offices, etc.
They are carrying on the struggle in 276 commune team farms,
forest areas, and tea plantations in the hsien and the town's
surrounding areas. The plan for sending educated youths up to
the mountains and down to the countryside from 1974 to 1980
will be known to every family and every home. The leaders of
the factory know the number of middle school graduates for that
factory each year and in which commune they are to be settled;
the village cadres and the poor and lower-middle peasants know
how many educated youths are coming in a particular year, and
from which units they are coming; parents know in which commune their sons and daughters will be settling when they have
graduated from middle school.

After factory-commune links have been formed and educated
youths have gone up to the mountains and down to the countryside to unite in the construction of socialism in the villages, the
undertaking becomes the work of the masses themselves, and
many problems are solved quickly by consultation between the
factory and the commune.

The Cadres Lead
the Teams

The Poor and Lower-
middle Peasants Reeducate
the Educated Youths

The educated youths on the farms, the forest stations, and the tea plantations have cadres to lead their teams and poor and lower-middle peasants to look after them.

The cadres who lead the teams are sent out by each factory to village commune teams according to their population. The requirements for being a team leader cadre are good political thought, a good manner of doing things, good health, and a certain amount of actual experience in struggle. At present, there are 193 selected team leader cadres in the town, of which 46 are women cadres. One hundred and seventy-six are Party members, 13 are Party Committee members of every level, and the rest are teachers and doctors. The parents understand these cadres and can trust them. Model team leader cadre Chu Chuan-fu of Pai-kuan Commune Pai-kuan Brigade forest area has been discussed and selected to be leader three times by the Hung-hsiang-chiang Machine Factory's workers and families; his work is outstanding, and he receives good comments from parents and educated youths.

The team leader cadres learn together, work together, and live together with the educated youths. They are the counselors who cultivate and teach the educated youths. Some of the team leader cadres take part in the work of the commune Party committee and the brigade Party branch; some take part in the work of small guidance groups for educated youth in the communes and brigades who have gone up to the mountains and down to the countryside. Frequently they brief the factory and the parents on the growth of the educated youths in the Three Great Revolutionary Movements and report to the commune team on their own work. This type of mutual communication helps factory and commune coordinate their work with educated youths. It also promotes mutual assistance between workers and peasants.

The poor and lower-middle peasants in the farms, forest

areas, and tea plantations are selected from each commune team. Some are former poor peasants, some are women cadres, some are demobilized soldiers, and there is a certain number of educated youths who have returned to the countryside. They are responsible for nurturing and teaching the educated youths, for leading the young people in production, and for helping the young people live a good life. In the farms, forest areas, and tea plantations of every commune team, generally about one third of the population are poor and lower-middle peasants. The responsible persons from the communes on the farms, forest areas, and tea plantations are mostly members of the commune Party committee or the secretaries of the brigade Party branch; the responsible person from the brigades on the farms, forest areas, or tea plantations is usually a deputy secretary of a brigade Party branch, or a hardworking leader of a production team.

The leading team cadres and the poor and lower-middle peasants mutually complement each other and together they cultivate and look after the educated youths. They say, "Chairman Mao has given us the responsibility of cultivating the educated youth, we must let each of these young people become a good successor to the revolution." The Lung-feng Commune Lung-feng Brigade forest farm has an educated youth named Hsiao-yü. One day he suddenly became seriously ill; eight poor and lower-middle peasants from the farm immediately carried Hsiao-yü, and hurrying through more than forty li, brought him to the health school at Chu-ting township. Late that night, Hsiao-yü's condition worsened and he urgently needed a blood transfusion. A poor peasant, old Ho Wan-nien, repeatedly begged the doctor to let him give his blood for Hsiao-yü, and the next night took Hsiao-yü by train to the hospital at Chu-chou, where he pulled through the crisis and recovered. Hsiao-yü was moved to the point of tears, and said, "The poor and lower-middle peasants are more loving than even my parents!"

Concentrating on the Farm   Settling in the Brigade

The farms, forest areas, and tea plantations of the commune

teams are set up on the principle of "three-level ownership with the team as the basis."* Within the scope of a brigade, the vast stretches of mountain land that the production team cannot cultivate on its own are managed by the brigade, which organizes production teams to cultivate it together. Within the scope of a commune, the vast stretches of mountain land that the brigade cannot cultivate on its own are managed by the commune, which organizes brigades to cultivate it together. The produce of the farms, forest areas, and tea plantations are proportionately divided according to whom the mountain land belongs to, the amount accumulated in each area, and the work contributions of each team. The educated youth who are settled in these commune teams make their homes with the production team and usually are on the farms studying and working. When the farming season is busy, they return to the team to help with production. Every month they return to the production team a few times to hold meetings and study with the commune members, constantly keeping in very close touch. Like the commune members who are living in the area, they share in the distribution with the production team members who are settled there.

The commune team farms, forest areas, and tea plantations are a great school. They not only have large areas for carrying out labor, they also provide very good conditions for the educated youth to learn and to live. The forest areas and tea plantations are flawlessly organized. Generally the commune farms, forest areas, and tea plantations have set up Party branches, Youth Corps branches, and revolutionary committees; the brigade farms, forest areas, and tea plantations have set up Party cells, Youth Corps cells, and farm committees; among the leading members there is always a specified proportion of educated youths. In the collective activities of the farm, the educated youths have comparatively more time to study politics and culture, and on the average they study about two hours a day; some farms even schedule a half day or a whole day every

---

*See the Glossary.

week for study. Many educated youths persist in writing for
self-improvement, writing diaries, producing wall newspapers,
studying Marxism, and criticizing revisionism. They have also
developed physical activities, organized militia training, and
set up amateur literature and arts propaganda teams to create
and perform cultural programs. Their cultural lives are very
lively, attracting and motivating the young people of the villages
to develop cultural and physical activities.

The establishment of commune team farms, forest areas, and
tea plantations required a period of very hard work. The educated youths and the poor and lower-middle peasants were a
dynamic force, emulating the Tachai model by terracing hills,
creating forests, and planting tea. Since last year, the commune
teams in which the educated youth are situated, through the concerted hard work of the poor and lower-middle peasants and the
educated youths, have created more than 12,000 mou of lumber
and orchard trees, cultivated more than 32 mou of young trees,
and revived large areas of decayed forest, and thus established
a new foundation for cash crops. They have also organized a
small group for scientific research, and among the things they
are experimenting with are catalpa tree seedlings, fir tree
planting and cultivation, grafting of orange trees, enrichment
of soil, control of rice insects, and so on. As a first step they
have achieved results in fourteen experiments. The poor and
lower-middle peasants, seeing the fir trees covering the mountain slopes in every direction, row upon row, and then seeing
the educated youth, themselves so much like fir trees, straight
and outstanding, cry out happily: "How good it is to have educated youths coming to the countryside! With them here, the
appearance of our village will change even more quickly!"

The educated youths, after being tempered in the commune
team farms, forest areas, and tea plantations, have undergone
deep changes in their thinking and their feeling. A group of
educated youths who settled in the Wang-shih-wan Commune
Hsien-feng Brigade forest area felt restless when they first
came, saying, "Mountains when you look up; mountains when
you go out; it's boring in the villages." Now they say, "You

look at the mountains and find that they are green; you look at
the sky and find that it is wide; the wide expanse of sky and
earth is great without end, and the poor and lower-middle peasants are each as close as relatives." Last year, among the
educated youths from the town who went to the countryside,
12 have already joined the Party, 791 have entered the Youth
Corps, and 492 have participated in leadership groups on every
level of the commune and brigade.

| Town and Country Com- | Jointly Solve the Prob- |
| plement Each Other | lems of Settlement |

Both the town and villages make up to the mountains and down
to the countryside work their own affair, and thus the practical
problems of the educated youths are solved quickly and well.
For example, the problem of housing: at the beginning of last
year, only 30 percent of the educated youths who went to the
countryside from Chu-chou had new houses to live in. After
factory-commune links were formed, the workers of the factory
and the poor and lower-middle peasants enthusiastically helped
the educated youths build living quarters. When the building
materials were insufficient, the factory satisfactorily used its
old materials; when problems of transportation came up, the
associated factory would send trucks out to help. The poor and
lower-middle peasants of Hsin-min Brigade of Wang-shih-wan
Commune, Chu-chou hsien, struggled day and night, and put up
houses by the light of lanterns and fire torches to enable the educated youths to move into their new quarters as soon as possible. The factory associated with this brigade, the provincial
equipment installation company, sent out trucks to transport
roof tiles from more than a hundred li away to the brigade. In
this way, in only twelve and a half days more than 15 units were
constructed, with more than 530 square meters of living space.
The educated youths, to express their resolution, used white
porcelain tiles in a house to inlay four large words: "Determined to Be in the Villages." Last year, in less than eight
months, Chu-chou hsien and the surrounding area of Chu-chou

constructed for the educated youths 957 housing units. More
than 95 percent of the educated youths moved into the new
housing. The average living space per person is 12.6 square
meters. Each commune team farm, forest area and tea plantation has its collective dining room, bathroom, pigpen, etc.;
some have even built a collective recreation room and installed
lights and running water. Some of the parents of the educated
youths were uneasy at first about their children's living arrangements, but when they came to the countryside to have a look,
they were very happy: "Ah, what a good thing it is to be a
peasant!"

To solve the problems of livelihood and self-sufficiency of
the educated youth who have gone to the countryside, the factory
and commune teams chose several positive measures to help
the educated youths develop production, increase income, and
justly record merits. The educated youths who went to the
countryside from the town were given food rations and other
income of about the same amount as the average for the commune members. To help the educated youths to establish a
good collective dining room, each commune team helped the
educated youths to develop many kinds of production — raising
pigs, chickens, ducks, fish, etc. — and set aside a certain amount
of field area for the young people to plant vegetables, thus
achieving basic self-reliance in supplementary foods. Because
of the special physiology of the female educated youths, each
commune brigade farm, forest area and tea plantation has
stipulated that during vacations young educated women will not
be scheduled to do heavy labor; some factories even send out
female worker committee members to talk to the female educated youths about personal hygiene matters.

Most of the educated youths have joined the production brigade's cooperative medical clinic. Some of the factory hospitals
help the farms, forest areas and tea plantations train educated
youths to be barefoot doctors. Some of the farms, forest areas,
and tea plantations plant Chinese medical herbs to resolve medical problems through self-reliance.

To cater to the educated youths' spiritual needs, the factories

started workers' committees, Communist Youth League [cells],
and women workers' committees to give the educated youths
works by Marx and Lenin and works by Chairman Mao, as well
as other study materials. The village commune teams help the
educated youths order newspapers and magazines and set up
broadcasting loudspeakers. The farms, forest areas, and tea
plantations where the educated youths are settled have almost
all built reading rooms, with a total of more than twenty thousand volumes of different types of reading materials. The broad
masses of educated youths feel comfortable politically, satisfied
in their lives, and happy in their work. They more and more
ardently love the new socialist villages.

Deep and Far-reaching Consequences

After the formation of factory-commune links, the educated
youths were like a cord binding city and village, workers and
peasants, in a close relationship. In the past, the peasants very
seldom went to the factory; now, when the village people go into
town, they often go to the factory to take a look, or go to the
educated youth's homes to talk a bit; the workers and cadres of
the town also often use their holidays to go to the villages, to
visit the poor and lower-middle peasants, to visit their own
children, and to take a look at the production situation in the
team. When some piece of machinery in the commune brigade
breaks down, it can be repaired on the spot. The workers and
the peasants become like brothers and relatives. In the past,
some of the factories looked upon helping the agriculture industry as "an extra burden"; now that too is changed. The
workers of the Chu-chou chemical factory say, "The poor and
lower-middle peasants bitterly struggle to make many contributions to the country, and also worry themselves about educating our youths; we must make a great effort to support agriculture." Last year they produced for the state more than
5,000 tons of chemical fertilizer over their quota to help agricultural production. Once, the rice of Huang-lung Commune was
infested by insects, and when the Chu-chou electrical factory

that is associated with it heard the news, it immediately sent
out seven electrical workers to help. They continuously struggled for two days and nights and put in more than three hundred
hei-kuang lamps in time to destroy the insect infestation and
guarantee a rich agricultural harvest. Last summer more than
20,000 workers from the town went to each commune team in
the hsien and municipal suburbs to participate in a joint effort.
They organized many agricultural-aid groups for village inspection towns to repair farm machinery and to advise the agricultural technicians. Each factory and mine also frequently sent
out movie groups and performing groups to the associated
commune team to show movies and to perform, enlivening the
village cultural life.

The massive help sent out by the factories increased the rate
of mechanization of agriculture. Each of the 35 communes in
Chu-chou hsien and the municipal suburbs has established farm
machinery repair shops. All have trucks and all brigades are
connected by public highways. The poor and lower-middle peasants are moved to say, "Formation of links between factories
and communes is good. The big change in our farming villages
cannot be separated from the help that elder-brother workers
have given us. We want to sell our best crops to the country;
we want to be able to give even more supplementary agricultural goods to the cities." Last year, Chu-chou hsien and the suburbs sold to the state 36 percent more surplus grain than in
the previous year, more than twice as many eggs, 35 percent
more fish, 36 percent more hot peppers, 7 times as many
watermelons, and 15 times as many oranges. In the past, some
factories have had to drive a car to the countryside to buy vegetables; now vegetables are plentiful in all seasons. A large
proportion of Chu-chou's workers are northerners, and love to
eat onions, so the commune team racked its wits to figure out
a method of transplanting spring onions from the north. Now
the markets of Chu-chou are already selling locally grown
onions.

*   *   *

Today in Chu-chou, Chairman Mao's great directive about educated youths going up to the mountains and down to the countryside has already entered deeply into the people's hearts. "To go to the countryside and engage in agriculture" has already become the prevalent attitude in society. The masses of parents enthusiastically support their sons and daughters becoming new peasants. The village poor and lower-middle peasants build spacious new houses and warmly welcome the new commune members. The educated youths who have already gone down to the countryside send out a ringing statement: Support the villages; build up the villages. Here, everywhere, is a sight to gladden hearts!

> Chinese Communist Party
> Chu-chou Committee
> Investigation Subcommittee
> Hunan Daily reporter

Consolidate and Develop the Achievements in up to the Mountains and down to the Countryside

Ch'i Chien*

Since the start of the Great Proletarian Cultural Revolution, tens of millions of educated youths, in response to Chairman Mao's call, have gone up to the mountains and down to the countryside in a gigantic revolutionary flow. This drive bears far-reaching significance for combating and preventing revisionism, reducing the three great differences, restricting bourgeois rights and bringing up millions of successors to the cause of the proletarian revolution. Spurred by the movement to study theory of the proletarian dictatorship, we must further consolidate and carry forward the great achievements in the movement up to the mountains and down to the countryside.

Chairman Mao's call that "educated youths must go to the villages and receive reeducation from the poor and lower-middle peasants" shows the vast group of educated young people in our country the direction of their advance. The movement of educated youths from the cities to the countryside is a delightful step they have made along the bright road of going up to the mountains and down to the countryside indicated by Chairman Mao. The first step is great, but things even greater will come after. Content merely with the step educated youths have made

*Ch'i Chien, "K'ung-ku ho fa-chan shang-shan hsia-hsiang ti ch'eng-kuo." Hung-ch'i [Red Flag] No. 7 (July 1, 1975), 6-9.

160

from cities to the countryside, some comrades regard the fulfillment of "mobilization" as completion of their work in this
movement. This is a wrong idea. Chairman Mao has said that
"there are still many obstacles and difficulties along the road
of revolution." The movement of educated youths up to the
mountains and down to the countryside is a profound revolution,
which cannot but meet with obstacles and difficulties. Every
step forward goes through a severe test of the struggle between
two classes, two lines, and two ideologies. Therefore, we must
wholeheartedly support the educated youths' unswerving advance
along the road leading up to the mountains and down to the
countryside. Many comrades have put it well: "Wherever the
educated youths go, our work of going up to the mountains and
down to the countryside, our support and concern, will follow
them there." This is an extremely responsible attitude toward
up-to-the-mountains and down-to-the-countryside work and de-
serves our praise. It demonstrates the color proper to a revolutionary cadre.

To consolidate and carry forward the achievements made in
the movement up to the mountains and down to the countryside,
a lot of work needs to be done by all fronts and all departments.
However, some comrades hold that since the educated youths
have already gone down to the countryside, the task of consolidation is transferred to the rural areas. This is a mistaken
view of separating mobilization from consolidation. The consolidation and development of the achievements in rustication is a
matter of paramount importance to the whole Party. It should
be performed under the unified leadership of the Party and with
backing from all sides of society. Party organs in the countryside and comrades working in the rural areas should take responsibility for the work. And urban Party organs and comrades
working in the cities should also do the same. In recent years,
some cities organized government cadres to visit the villages
where educated youths stayed. They conducted investigations
and gave comfort to the rusticated youths, and joined forces
with local Party organs and poor and lower-middle peasants in
an effort to consolidate the rustication work. They not only

toured the villages and inquired after the educated youths household by household, but also made careful and penetrating survey and study. They helped solve some immediate, practical difficulties currently facing the educated youths, while at the same time attempting to tackle some fundamental problems in long-range perspective. At present, departments of industry, finance and commerce, culture and education in some provinces and municipalities have already put on their agenda the work of consolidating and carrying forward the achievements in the movement up to the mountains and down to the countryside. This action is worthy and should be advocated. Apart from enthusiastically fulfilling the task of turning out products in support of agriculture according to the state plan, some industry departments take inventory of their warehouses and dig out resources so that they can implement the Party and state policy of rendering material support in a planned way to rural areas, especially areas where rusticated youths are concentrated. There are cities which dispatch workers to the countryside to help the educated youths learn to repair and make machines, cultivating their technical ability. Some commerce departments assist areas where rusticated youths are concentrated to develop diversified economy and keep the channels of production, supply, and sales open. And some departments of culture, education, and publication actively run correspondence courses for the rusticated youths, publish youth self-study series of books, conduct scientific farming experiments, and so on. These endeavors win the warm approval of rusticated youths. Comrades of all fronts, let us all seriously think it over: In consolidating and carrying forward the achievements in the movement up to the mountains and down to the countryside and in showing concern for the growth of educated youths, what have we done? And what do we still have to do?

Some comrades are merely content with "welcoming" the educated youths into the villages. When the salute of drums and gongs comes to a stop, and the youths have been registered and scheduled for labor, these comrades think their task is over. This attitude is as wrong as that of grasping only "mobilization" mentioned earlier. It would be even more wrong to consider the rusticated youths a "burden" and regard the task as an "extra load." The passive attitude of these comrades is often closely related to their lack of correct understanding of the educated youths. Chairman Mao said: "The young people are the most active and vital force in society. They are the most eager to learn and the least conservative in their thinking. This is especially so in the era of socialism." The broad masses of educated youths have a potentially inexhaustible enthusiasm for socialism. They are full of vigor and ambition, resolved to reduce the three great differences and to restrict bourgeois rights. This is the essence of the matter, the main current. However, there is another aspect: Owing to the influence of bourgeois ideology and the force of petty bourgeois habits, and especially because of the ingratiation and corruption of the class enemy, problems of one kind or another may arise among the rusticated youths. If we have these problems in sight and make Marxist analysis of them, we will realize more than ever the heavy responsibility on our shoulders for doing a good job of up-to-the-mountains and down-to-the-countryside work. Owing to their lack of political experience and experience of social life, quite a few young people are still rather naïve. But naïveté can grow into maturity. We should regard all rusticated youths as young seedlings and intensively care for and cultivate them. As a matter of fact, wherever the local Party organizations attach great importance to rustication work, educated youths there will make rapid progress and play a significant part in the Three Great Revolutionary Movements. As a matter of fact, these young people are not a "burden" but a valuable force in the cause of revolution. In places where rustication work is poorly done, the educated youths there will be prevented from displaying their revolutionary enthusiasm. It is a reflection that the socialist position of that place is not consolidated and the evil trends of capitalism grow rampant. Therefore, Party organizations in the rural areas, particularly Party committees at the <u>hsien</u> and commune levels, should integrate the work of rustication with the consolidation of socialist positions in the countryside. They must show concern for the growth of the rusticated youths in various respects, including politics, production and life.

To consolidate and carry forward the achievements in the movement up to the mountains and down to the countryside calls for our wholehearted warmth toward the educated youths. It exacts painstaking effort from the cadres. A Party secretary of a hsien committee has put it well: "When educated youths put their whole lives at the Party's disposal, Party organizations at various levels should do a good job in arranging their lives." This requires us not only being concerned with the political progress and improvement of the study of the rusticated youths but also making good arrangements for their production and livelihood in accordance with local conditions. We should not only care about their present situation, but also take into account what lies in their future. Here we cite the case of Tingnan hsien in Kiangsi Province as an example. This hsien is located in the mountainous area in south Kiangsi. Formerly the rusticated youths were scattered in different production teams. Through investigation and study, and extensively soliciting opinions from educated youths and poor and lower-middle peasants, comrades of the hsien Party committee became aware that in light of local conditions the scattered deployment of rusticated youths was not appropriate and a relative concentration would be advisable. Through experiments, they adopted a method of proper concentration and set up youth production brigades and youth farms under collective ownership. The departments concerned extended to the young people the necessary material support. Guided by the policy of "taking food grain as the key link, strive for all-around development," these youth brigades and farms, based on the local conditions of having a lot of mountains, scarce fields, and abundant forest resources, engaged both in farming production and diversified economy. Where conditions permit, they have set up small factories and handicraft workshops so that they can do farm work during the busy farming season and do industrial work in the slack season. These kinds of youth brigades and farms have many advantages. As the educated youths are comparatively concentrated, it is more convenient for Party organs to strengthen the leadership and organize the youths for unified study. With young people of different conditions fighting together, they can bring into full play their respective specialties. Even those who are physically weak can have jobs they are able to do. Pooling together to build brigades and farms, the young people lead a collective life and have meals at the mess hall without planting private lots, and their awareness of collectivism is reinforced more than ever. After one or two years of hard battle, some youth brigades and farms have doubled their grain output and made considerable progress in sideline production as well. In this way, they have not only created necessary conditions for developing and enhancing the collective economy of the communes and brigades, but also increase their own income and lessen the burden on their families and society. Part of the youth brigades and farms plan to draw some money from their collective accumulated funds to build new agricultural villages or establish a depository so that favorable conditions can be created to meet the practical needs of their daily lives. Ting-nan hsien has a rather good method of organizing the rusticated youths; however, it requires certain conditions. Besides, other effective forms have also been tried elsewhere in accordance with local conditions. No matter what form is adopted, the socialist initiative of rusticated youths can be brought into full play as long as they are guided by a correct line. They can be guided to rely on their own resources and wage arduous struggle so that our countryside will become a vast universe for them to develop their talents to the fullest.

Having millions of educated youths going up to the mountains and down to the countryside is a strategic measure the proletariat takes in exercising an overall dictatorship over the bourgeoisie, making it impossible for the latter to survive or reemerge. Some of our comrades regard rustication work as an "extra load," the root cause of which is that they fail to fully understand the significance embodied in this socialist new thing. They always feel that they are already fully occupied with rural work, which is so complicated and pressing, and simply cannot afford to handle and solve the problems arising from the rustication of educated youths. To contradict rustication with other tasks in the rural areas is a metaphysical point of view. These comrades tend to keep in sight the various concrete jobs confronting them but fail to see the indispensability of the educated youths in the drive to modernize and mechanize the countryside. They are blind to the fact that the upbringing of millions of successors to the revolutionary cause of the proletariat is a one-hundred-year plan for consolidating the proletarian dictatorship. Precisely because they overlook the significance of this major issue, they are led to regard the work as an "extra load." We hope these comrades who do not yet take the rustication work seriously will conscientiously study the theory of proletarian dictatorship so that they can make a leap in their understanding and realize a remarkable change in their action.

The study of the theory of the proletarian dictatorship serves as a strong impetus to consolidate and develop the achievements made in the movement up to the mountains and down to the countryside. Chairman Mao pointed out: "Why did Lenin speak of exercising dictatorship over the bourgeoisie? It is essential to get this question clear. Lack of clarity on this question will lead to revisionism." Millions of educated youths settling down in the countryside are bound to restrict effectively bourgeois rights, reduce the three great differences, and root out the soil which engenders capitalism and new bourgeois elements. At present, the broad masses of the rusticated youths are earnestly studying the theory of the proletarian dictatorship and have greatly enhanced their consciousness of putting down deep roots in the countryside. They express their will to behave like tough pine trees and to remain permanently in the countryside despite the lashings of wind and rain. They declare: The concept of "study well to be officials" advocated by Confucius cannot allure us; Lin Piao's paradox of "disguised labor through reform" cannot shake our determination. This demonstrates that to deepen the study of the theory of the proletarian dictatorship will serve as a mighty impetus in the drive to rusticate educated youths.

In order to consolidate and carry out the achievements made

in the movement up to the mountains and down to the countryside, it is essential to organize the rusticated youths to conscientiously study Marxism-Leninism and works by Chairman
Mao and to acquire a good grasp of the theory of the proletarian
dictatorship so that they can ceaselessly raise their consciousness of putting down deep roots in the countryside. We must encourage them to challenge bravely the concepts of bourgeois
rights and thoroughly break away from traditional selfish ideas.
We must deal resolute blows at the class enemies who perpe-
trate criminal acts to undermine the rustication drive.

Along the bright road of going down to the countryside as indicated by Chairman Mao, millions of educated youths are forg-
ing forward with gigantic strides. It is an irresistible trend of
history. Let all of us support this great initiative!

Twelve Million Educated Youths
Gloriously Engage in Agriculture

People's Daily*

[Excerpts] Peking, 22 December — Since Chairman Mao's
1968 call for educated youths to go to the rural areas, wave
after wave of educated young people throughout the country have
whipped up a large scale movement to go to the countryside.
Since the Great Proletarian Cultural Revolution began, 12 million educated youths have settled in the countryside. This is a
fruitful result of the Great Proletarian Cultural Revolution as
well as a brilliant victory for Chairman Mao's revolutionary
line in the youth movement.

This year, under the guidance of Chairman Mao's series of
important instructions on sturying theory to combat and prevent revisionism, on promoting stability and unity and on boost-
ing the national economy, a total of 2 million educated youths
in our country have settled in the countryside to take the road
of integrating with workers and peasants. More educated youths
have gone to the countryside this year than in any recent year,
and better settlement work has been done this year than ever
before. Party organizations have effectively strengthened their

*"I-ch'ien erh-pai wan chih-shih ch'ing-nien kuang-jung wu-
nung." Jen-min jih-pao [People's Daily], December 23,
1975. These excerpts are taken, with minor editorial re-
visions, from Foreign Broadcast Information Service, No. 248
(December 24, 1975).

leadership and have assigned more than 60,000 cadres to lead educated youths to the countryside to help the rural communes settle them. They have linked the work of settling educated youths in the countryside with the movement to learn from Tachai so as to enable educated youths to display their important role in this movement. Since the beginning of this year, 15 provinces, municipalities and autonomous regions have held congresses of advanced collectives and individuals among educated youths in which about 20,000 representatives were commended....

Settling educated youths in the countryside is an important event in socialist revolution and construction. This is of profound significance in hastening the building of modern socialist agriculture, combating and preventing revisionism, consolidating the dictatorship of the proletariat and training and bringing up millions of successors to the revolutionary cause of the proletariat. This great revolutionary movement has developed in the fierce struggle between the two lines. As early as in the period of agricultural cooperation, Chairman Mao pointed out: "All people who have had some education ought to be very happy to work in the countryside if they get the chance. In our vast rural areas, there is plenty of room for them to develop their talents to the full." After that, many educated youths, in warm response to Chairman Mao's call and full of pride and enthusiasm, went to the vast rural areas. However, because Liu Shao-ch'i vigorously pushed a revisionist line and made great efforts to preach such fallacies as 'study to become an official,' 'go to the countryside to gain credit' and 'cultivate yourself behind closed doors' to obstruct and sabotage educated youths' integration with workers and peasants, only a few more than 1.2 million educated youths went to the countryside during the 10 years or so between the beginning of agricultural cooperation and the beginning of the Great Proletarian Cultural Revolution.

The Great Proletarian Cultural Revolution smashed the bourgeois headquarters headed by Liu Shao-ch'i and criticized the counterrevolutionary revisionist line, especially after the Peo-

ple's Daily published Chairman Mao's important instruction on
December 22, 1968, that "educated youths must go to the villages and be reeducated by the poor and lower-middle peasants.
We must persuade the cadres and others in the cities to send
their sons and daughters who have graduated from lower-middle
schools, upper-middle schools, and universities to the countryside and make it a campaign. Comrades from villages everywhere should welcome them." The masses and cadres warmly
responded to this call by Chairman Mao and launched a vigorous
movement throughout the country to settle educated youths in
the countryside. In 1969 alone, 2.7 million educated youths went
to the countryside.... In the Three Great Revolutionary Movements millions of educated youths have faced the world and
braved the storm, striven to study Marxism-Leninism-Mao
Tsetung Thought and modestly received reeducation from the
poor and lower-middle peasants. They have learned what they
could not learn from school and have enhanced their awareness
of class struggle and the struggle between the two lines. By the
end of 1974 more than 70,000 educated youths had joined the
Party, more than 1.48 million have joined the League, and more
than 290,000 had been elected to leading posts.

To train successors to the revolutionary cause, many Party
organizations have sent educated youths to backward brigades
in recent years to let them be tempered there.... Last year,
Kai-yuan hsien, Liaoning, sent more than 200 outstanding educated youths to backward brigades to shoulder heavy burdens.
... They have helped these backward units transform their
people, land, and production....

The training and education by Party organizations and the
poor and lower-middle peasants and the arduous manual labor
in the Three Great Revolutionary Movements in the rural areas
have greatly helped the younger generation remold their world
outlook. Many educated youths have opened barren lands and
blazed trails in remote localities. They have worked very hard
to create a new world.

In 1973, 60 educated youths came to Ta-chuang-tzu Commune
in Chin-ta hsien, Kansu. Outside the Great Wall in the Gobi

Desert, despite bitter winds and dust storms, these educated
youths, together with commune members, opened 1,500 mou of
barren land and produced 430,000 chin of grain in the spring of
1974. This year they produced 600,000 chin. In 1970 more than
400 educated youths from Peking, Shanghai, Mu-tan-chiang and
Chi-hsi came to the No. 12 Branch of the Shan-ho farm in Heilungkiang. Over the past few years, together with farm workers,
they have opened 30,000 mou of barren land, built water con-
servation projects involving 580,000 cubic meters of earth and
stone work, planted more than 439,000 trees and produced 11.68
million chin of grain for the state....

The vast rural areas are a university for educated youths.
There is an inexhaustible amount of knowledge for them to
learn and numberless tasks for them to do. Many educated
youths produced inventions and creations in the practice of the
Three Great Revolutionary Movements....

The victorious results achieved by the vast numbers of educated youths in the countryside are a warm ode to Chairman
Mao's revolutionary line and a forceful repudiation of argu-
ments against new socialist things. At present, strong public
opinion supports and maintains this new socialist thing. Revolutionary parents employ the new idea of "raising children to
prevent revisionism" and "sending children to rural areas to
work on farms" to replace the old traditions and conceptions
of "raising children to provide for old age" and "hoping for a
bright future for their children."...

Because integrating educated youths with workers and peasants is a challenge to age-old habits and traditions, it is not an
easy undertaking. The struggle between the two lines involved
in this new thing will go on for a long time. The current heated
debate on the educational front concerns not only the problem
of revolution in education but also the orientation of the youth
movement. The essence of the struggle is the major issue of
whether we should bring up successors to the revolutionary
cause of the proletariat or raise intellectual aristocrats for
the bourgeoisie. In the face of this struggle between right and
wrong, the more than 10 million educated youths who have set-

tled in the countryside are a tremendous force for carrying out and defending Chairman Mao's proletarian revolutionary line. They have used their personal experience to refute those absurd remarks appearing on the educational front and are determined to march forward bravely along the road of integrating with the workers and peasants pointed out by Chairman Mao and use their concrete deeds to consolidate and develop the fruits of the Great Proletarian Cultural Revolution so as to build our country into a strong, modern socialist country.

Have a Warm Concern for the Growth of Married Educated Youths Who Have Gone down to the Countryside

An Investigative Report
of Hai-ch'eng Hsien*

"People's Daily" Editor's Note

Showing warm concern for the growth of resettled educated youths who are married is an aspect of our endeavor to resettle educated youths in the countryside. It
is a matter deserving our attention. Party organizations at various levels in Hai-ch'eng hsien are imbued
with a lofty sense of political duty. They hold themselves completely responsible for the well-being of the
resettled educated young people and have laid great emphasis on doing this work well. Their experience can
be consulted as reference.

As some resettled educated youths grow older, it is
necessary to guide them in correctly handling the problem of marriage. We must encourage the resettled
youths to take the lead in practicing late marriage,
which will in turn serve as a strong impetus to reforming the old custom of getting married early. After the
young people get married, we must educate them to adhere to the principle of planned birth and help them

---

*Hai-ch'eng hsien ti tiao-ch'a pao-kao. "Je-ch'ing kuan-huai
i-hun hsia-hsiang chih-shih ch'ing-nien ti ch'eng-chang." Jen-
min jih-pao [People's Daily], November 23, 1974.

173

make good arrangements for political studies, productive labor, and their home lives. When all this is done
successfully, we can better encourage the broad masses
of educated youth to persist in the countryside and allow
them to develop their talents to the full in the vast rural
areas.

* * *

Pursuant to Chairman Mao's instruction that "new China
must care for her youth and show concern for the growth of the
younger generation," Party organizations at various levels in
Hai-ch'eng hsien of Liaoning Province have engaged in a serious effort to do a good job with educated youths who have gone
up to the mountains and down to the countryside. They treat
married and unmarried educated youths alike, paying attention
to helping them politically so that they can raise their awareness of class struggle and two-line struggle. They also help
the married young people solve certain practical problems in
their daily lives. With their help, the married youths are reinforced in their determination to persist in the countryside
and continue to play a positive role in the Three Great Revolutionary Movements.

I

Hai-ch'eng hsien has received, since 1968, more than forty-
eight thousand educated youths from urban areas. Led by Party
organizations at different levels and reeducated by the poor and
lower-middle peasants, the broad masses of educated youths
persist in the countryside and are sturdily maturing. In recent
years a number of resettled educated youths have gotten married in the rural areas and prepared to settle there for life.

In the autumn of 1973, one resettled educated youth who was
already married wrote to the hsien Party committee, saying:
"Cadres in our team no longer treat us married young people
as educated youths resettled in the countryside. They do not

ask us to participate in theoretical studies and political activities conducted at the youth point [ch'ing-nien tien]. And they
show little interest in our lives and productive labor." This
letter made the hsien Party committee realize that showing
concern for the growth of resettled educated youths who are
married has become a new issue in our endeavor to resettle
educated young people in the countryside. We must be highly
attentive to the problem. As more and more resettled educated
youths will get married in rural areas from now on, it will become increasingly important for us to show concern for the
growth of married educated youths.

In order to acquire firsthand information in this matter, the
Party committee of Hai-ch'eng hsien sent the secretary in
charge of the work among resettled educated youths, and comrades from relevant departments to visit personally the production team where the writer of the letter stayed. There they
made further inquiries into the case and helped him solve the
problem. Following this, these comrades toured the countryside to conduct more investigations and studies and sum up experiences and lessons. Through investigation, they found that
cadres in a certain brigade of Wang-shih Commune were of the
opinion that "since the married resettled educated youths will
move out of the youth point after marriage, it is no longer
necessary for us to get involved with them." Because of this,
they showed little concern for the political studies and livelihood
of these young people. As a result, certain married educated
youths developed an uneasy feeling and vacillated in their determination to stay in the countryside. Contrary to the attitude
of cadres in this brigade, the Party branch of the No. 2 Brigade
in Niu-chuang Commune showed great concern for resettled
young people who were married. The secretary of the Party
branch visited the married young people of the entire brigade
many times. He encouraged them to read and study earnestly
and to participate actively in collective productive labor. He
also helped them solve such practical problems as housing,
getting babysitters, etc. After her marriage, a resettled educated young woman by the name of Ch'en Chüan had always been

in pursuit of political advancement. The Party organization helped her grow and allowed her to temper herself in the forefront of class struggle. She made rapid progress and soon was admitted into the Party. She was then appointed to be secretary of the brigade Party branch. In her brigade, educated youths who are married feel the deep concern of Chairman Mao and the Party Central Committee and enjoy the best of care from the Party Organization and from the poor and lower-middle peasants. One after another they resolved to persist in the countryside so as to play an even greater role in the Three Revolutionary Movements.

Two different attitudes yield two different results, a fact which the Hai-ch'eng hsien Party committee found highly instructive. At the beginning of this year, the hsien Party committee called a meeting devoted to a serious discussion of this problem. The conferees all agreed that for the educated youths to get married in the countryside, settle there, and establish a home is a major achievement in the movement to send educated youths up to the mountains and down to the countryside. Showing concern for the growth of educated youths who are already married will greatly enhance the educated youths' determination to persist in the countryside and follow the road of integrating themselves with worker and peasant masses as indicated by Chairman Mao. It bears great significance to the undertaking of training successors to the revolutionary cause of the proletariat. The hsien Party committee has held three successive discussion meetings participated in by representatives of resettled educated youths who are already married. The Party committee extensively solicited opinions and issued special directives, calling Party organizations at all levels to concern themselves with the growth of those married young people. Leaders in the hsien Party committee strive to set an example by their own conduct. Every time they go to the countryside on business, they visit the married young people on their way and try to find out how things stand with them. If any problem surfaces, they immediately help find a solution. Party organizations at the commune and brigade levels also place this work on their agendas. Generally, they each call a discussion meeting participated in by married educated youths. On many occasions, quite a number of communes have dispatched work teams to check the implementation of the required work from brigade to brigade and household to household. Cadres in that brigade in Wang-shih Commune who had previously neglected work among married educated youths have also changed their attitude. With the help of the hsien Party committee, they have raised their awareness of two-line struggle. The secretary of the brigade Party branch said: "When educated youths get married, it does not mean that we have completed the job of reeducating them. We must hold ourselves completely responsible for their political advancement and strive to train them to be successors to the revolutionary cause." The League organization, the Poor Peasants Association and the Women's Committee of this brigade all voluntarily join forces with the Party branch in a coordinated effort to show warm concern from all sides for the growth of the resettled married educated youths.

II

Party organizations at various levels in Hai-ch'eng hsien put primary emphasis on showing concern for married young people from an ideological and political perspective. They guide them in assiduously studying works of Marxism-Leninism and works by Chairman Mao and have them take an active part in the movement to criticize Lin Piao and Confucius so that they can incessantly enhance their awareness of class struggle and two-line struggle. Party organizations at all levels in the entire hsien presented to the resettled educated youths, both married and unmarried, works of Marxism-Leninism and works by Chairman Mao. Many leading comrades of Party committees at the commune level frequently visit the households of the married young people in order to help them with difficult problems arising from their studies. With the assistance from Party organizations at different levels, the married educated

youths in the entire hsien have formed themselves into more than
one hundred study groups in pursuit of Marxist theory. And
each group has worked out its own study plan. Up to now, they
have mostly studied six works of Marxism-Leninism and works
by Chairman Mao, including the Communist Manifesto, Critique
of the Gotha Program, and "On the Correct Handling of Contradictions among the People." Some of the educated youths have
read the Selected Works of Lenin and Selected Works of Mao
Tse-tung and have taken many notes. When political studies are
conducted at youth points, married resettled youth are included.

   After resettled educated youths get married, they are likely
to encounter certain ideological problems arising from the
change in their lives and environment. Therefore, Party organizations at various levels in Hai-ch'eng hsien continue their
efforts to strengthen the reeducation of the married young people. Yao Su-fang, an educated youth in Ta-hsin Brigade of Pa-li
Commune, serves as the brigade forecaster of insect pests.
After she was married, she once harbored the mistaken idea
that since she was already settled in the countryside, all she
had to do was to manage the affairs in her little family well. As
a result of her attitude, the forecasting work in her brigade was
affected. For the purpose of helping her set a far-reaching goal
of revolution for herself, the secretary of the brigade Party
branch held three heart-to-heart talks with her and sent her to
attend the theoretical studies class run by the commune. Gradually she came to realize that educated youths should not regard
their marriage in the countryside as an end to their reeducation
by the poor and lower-middle peasants. They must continue
their efforts to temper themselves and strive to play a positive
role in the Three Great Revolutionary Movements, contributing
their share to revamping the backward look in the countryside.
If one is only engrossed in one's little home life, one will certainly fall short of the expectations of the Party and the poor
and lower-middle peasants. From that time onward, little Yao
handled the relationship between household chores and her work
correctly, earnestly engaging herself in making insect pest
forecasts. Last year, the sorghum in her brigade suffered an

attack of aphids, which hit the area like a violent wave. Production teams subordinate to the brigade prepared to spread
out all their people for extensive prevention and control.
Through careful and penetrating investigation and tests, little
Yao found that the low-lying areas were the hardest hit and suggested that work forces be concentrated rather than be widely
deployed for a battle of annihilation against the insect. Because
the production teams followed her suggestion, they not only prevented the spread of the pestilence, but also saved over eleven
hundred dollars' worth of insecticide and a great amount of
labor for the brigade.

Certain resettled educated youths regard themselves as "permanent residents" in the village once they get married. They
think they will come to no good if they offend others, and they
dare not wage struggles as they did before their marriage. In
light of this situation, Party branches of many brigades guide
the married young people in a serious effort to study Chairman
Mao's theory of continuing revolution under the proletarian
dictatorship and the Party's basic line. They help the married
youths acquire a deep understanding that "the Communist philosophy is a philosophy of struggle" and organize them to participate in class struggle and two-line struggle in real life. For
example, the married youths were dispatched to certain backward units to help the Party organizations there with the movement to criticize Lin Piao and Confucius. They were required
to join forces with the poor and lower-middle peasants in
launching a mass movement to learn from Tachai in agriculture, and they were also asked to join theory study groups. In
showing concern for the political advancement of the married
educated youths, Party organizations at various levels admit,
in time, those who meet the qualification requirements for the
Party and the League.

III

Party organizations at various levels in Hai-ch'eng hsien
also pay attention to solving certain practical problems which

the resettled educated youths encounter in their married lives.
For the married educated youths, especially when both the male
and the female have been resettled in the countryside, the most
urgent problem to solve is the problem of housing. Starting
from the actual situation, the hsien Party committee and Party
organizations at the commune and brigade levels mainly resort
to two methods in solving the problem: (1) After brigades
throughout the hsien have set up educated youth points, the previous production team youth points are dissolved, and the houses
they vacate are assigned, on the basis of priority, to the married educated youths as their residences. (2) Based on the principle of "self-funding plus help from the masses and assistance
from the state," the married young people are organized in a
planned way to build houses on their own.

When the resettled young women get married and have children, they are likely to become entangled in household chores,
busy all day with feeding pigs, preparing meals, and carrying
babies. How can we help relieve this situation? Backed by the
hsien Party committee, many brigade Party branches have conducted classes for special studies, organizing the married young
educated women to study Chairman Mao's brilliant article "The
Direction of the Youth Movement." With this, they educated the
young women to continue the revolution without interruption, to
break completely from the old, traditional ideas and to take the
lead in practicing planned birth. A resettled young woman in
Hu-lu-yü of Mao-ch'i Commune had been very active during the
period when she was at the youth point. At that time she used
to take the initiative in everything, be it studies or farm labor.
After she was married and had a child, she thought that "she
was of no use any longer." In May of this year she attended a
discussion meeting of representatives of married educated
youths sponsored by the hsien Party committee and received
great encouragement from the meeting. Leaders from the hsien
and commune Party committees personally visited her at her
home, and the secretary of the brigade Party branch showed
concern for her as well. He encouraged her to continue her
effort in tempering and maturing herself through the Three

Great Revolutionary Movements and, at the same time, helped her solve certain practical problems. When the child hindered her, the brigade found an old grandma of poor peasant origin to babysit for her. When her child got sick, the brigade sent the barefoot doctor to provide medical treatment. All this moved her deeply, and from that time onward she regained her revolutionary initiative and kept a record of everyday attendance, month after month. Moreover, she got three other married educated young women organized. Together they persisted in taking part in theoretical studies and political activities. In order to solve the problem of babysitting, Pai-hai Brigade of Hsi-ssu Commune specially set up a day-care center for the married educated youths. Thus they are able to fight without worry in the forefront of learning from Tachai in agriculture.

People's Daily Correspondent
People's Daily Reporter

[The following is a supplement to the article above, and is based on a November 15, 1974, broadcast from Shen-yang in Liaoning — FBIS, No. 229 (November 26, 1974).]

[Excerpts] Party organizations at all levels in Hai-ch'eng hsien, Liaoning, are taking good care of the married educated young people settled in the countryside. They have taken effective measures to do good work with these young men and women.

Over the past few years, 1,631 young men and women among the educated young people in Hai-ch'eng hsien who have gone to the countryside have married and settled in the rural areas. In the past, the hsien Party committee and Party organizations of the communes and brigades failed to pay sufficient attention to married young intellectuals. Since the start of the movement to criticize Lin Piao and Confucius, the hsien Party committee has seriously listened to the views expressed by the married young intellectuals, solicited comments from the poor and lower-middle peasants, studied Chairman Mao's teachings on educated youth and related documents, together with the comrades of departments concerned, and penetratingly criticized the reactionary fallacies spread by Lin Piao and Confucius, that "one studies to become an official" and [going to the countryside] is "disguised labor reform." They have included work on married young intellectuals settling in the countryside on their agendas. They also feel that doing this work well is not only conducive to helping the married youths remain in the countryside to continue revolution in a better way, but also has profound and widespread influence on the unmarried educated youths settled in the countryside as well as on the whole of society.

Party organizations throughout the country therefore have first intensified political and ideological work among the married youths, leading them to study works by Marx, Lenin and Chairman Mao and to take an active part in the criticism movement.

Party organizations at all levels have conducted training and education among the educated young people — both married and unmarried — on an equal basis, treid to absorb into the Party and League advanced elements, and selected them to serve as cadres. Among the married educated youths, more than 40 have joined the Party after their marriage and some 100 have joined the leading groups at all levels. Party organizations at all levels have also used the Party's basic line in educating the married educated young people, encouraging them to persist in continuing the revolution and developing their talents to the fullest in the vast rural areas.

The hsien Party committee has also paid attention to advanced examples among the educated young couples. Also, Party organizations at all levels have helped the youths solve practical problems in their daily lives. If both the husband and the wife are educated young people settled in the countryside, they will be helped by the Party organizations in solving the problem of living quarters immediately after their marriage.

Party organizations at all levels have also paid attention to conducting education on late marriage and planned parenthood among the educated youths. All married young intellectuals in the <u>hsien</u> generally have adopted planned parenthood.

At present, necessary preparations are being made throughout the <u>hsien</u> to enable the educated youths settled in the countryside to live better during the winter.

Fully Develop the Role of Educated Youths in the Movement to Learn from Tachai in Agriculture

The CCP Committee of Hai-ch'eng
Hsien, Liaoning Province*

Twelve representatives of educated youths who had either
returned to or resettled in the countryside participated in the
National Conference for Learning from Tachai in Agriculture
and wrote "A Letter to Chairman Mao and the Party Central
Committee." We read that letter and thereby received a great
education. Educated young people are determined to charge to
the fore in the great revolutionary movement of learning from
Tachai in agriculture and dedicate their youth to its fulfillment.
We feel proud of them. We must create favorable conditions
for the young people so that they can bring into full play their
role in the movement to learn from Tachai in agriculture.

The movement to learn from Tachai in agriculture is closely
connected with the educated youths' endeavor to resettle in
the countryside and follow the road of integrating with the
poor and lower-middle peasants. Both aim to expedite the
building of a modernized socialist agriculture, narrowing
the three great differences, preventing and combating revisionism and consolidating the proletarian dictatorship. Learning
from Tachai in agriculture is another great revolutionary

*Chung-kung Liao-ning sheng Hai-ch'eng hsien wei-yüan-hui,
"Ch'ung-fen fa-hui chih-shih ch'ing-nien tsai nung-yeh hsüeh
Ta-chai chung ti tso-yung." Jen-min jih-pao [People's Daily],
October 31, 1975.

184

movement in our countryside that follows the movements of
land reform, agricultural cooperativization, and communization.
Only by enthusiastically plunging into this great revolution can
educated youths expect to receive a still better reeducation
from the poor and lower-middle peasants and truly develop
their talents to the full.

Pursuant to Chairman Mao's instruction that "comrades
from villages everywhere should welcome their going," our
hsien, over the past few years, has taken in more than fifty-six
thousand educated youths from urban areas. Under the guidance
of Chairman Mao's revolutionary line, the broad masses of educated youths have joined forces with the poor and lower-middle peasants in a determined effort to battle against nature and
learn from Tachai. They are resolved to take root in the countryside and have made satisfactory progress. Liu Li, an educated youth who has settled in Yü-kuan Brigade of Kan-wang
Commune, now holds the post of secretary of the commune
Party committee. The area where the commune is located was
hit by a strong earthquake this year. In a revolutionary spirit
that "one will not be weighed down even by Mount Tai," she led
the poor and lower-middle peasants and members of the entire
commune in fighting against the disaster by persistently mod-
eling themselves on the people of Tachai. However, the good
crops they raised after they had repaired the disastrous dam-
age caused by the quake were hit by a flood unprecedented in
many years. With the assistance of the senior Party secretary
Kuan T'ing-kuei, Liu Li stood in the turbulent waters and directed the battle against the flood. Having brought the disaster
under control, the commune eventually reaped a bountiful harvest. Several days ago, she plodded around scores of li on a
fact-finding tour and succeeded in drawing a blueprint for flood
control.

Inspired by the spirit of the National Conference for Learning from Tachai in Agriculture, the entire commune was engrossed in a joint battle for farmland capital construction. The
poor and lower-middle peasants said in delight: "Being tempered in the great storms of revolution, Liu Li has grown

sturdier than ever." At present, over three hundred production
teams, which account for one tenth of the total number of production teams in the entire hsien, are headed by resettled educated youths. During the movement to learn from Tachai in
agriculture, these young people did fine work and registered
rapid growth. The broad masses praised them as reliable
successors to the revolutionary cause of the proletariat.

In Hsi-ssu Commune there is an "August 28" Enterprise
Starting Team made up of educated young people. Encouraged
by the Tachai spirit, they reclaimed one hundred mou of waste
alkaline beach. At that time, they had to walk fifty-odd li every
day to reclaim the land. In a revolutionary spirit and with
heroic efforts, they succeeded in cultivating paddy rice on the
waste alkaline beach, and the per mou yield exceeded the target
set forth in the National Agricultural Development Program for
areas south of the Yangtze River. They gathered in a rich harvest in grain and achieved even more in terms of ideological
remolding. Urban factories made several recruitment efforts
in their area but they firmly decided not to return to the city.
Here is the militant poem they wrote:

> We bear in mind what Chairman Mao teaches us,
> And uphold the red flag of learning from Tachai.
> We resolve to take root in the countryside,
> And dedicate our fiery youth to the future.

In the course of struggle between two classes, two roads,
and two lines, the educated youths always take a clear-cut
stand. They daringly resist and combat the evil wind of capitalism and they are the least conservative in thinking when
conducting scientific experiments. As they are able to integrate cultural and scientific knowledge with practice in socialist agriculture, they have made remarkable achievements.
Educated youth Ko Ke-chien holds the post of deputy secretary
of the Party branch of Yü-kuan Brigade. He is an able person
with many skills. He serves simultaneously as an agricultural
technician, an electrician, and also a barefoot veterinarian.

Together with the poor and lower-middle peasants, he directed great effort to manufacturing bacterial fertilizer, which contributed to the increase of grain production.

Over the past few years we members of the hsien Party committee regarded the educated youths as the wealth of the Party. We showed great concern for them and employed them as a shock force. From now on we will continue to give free rein to the role of the educated youths in the movement for learning from Tachai in agriculture. In order to effectively transform the backward brigades and teams, we are preparing to take fifteen hundred educated youths for the task. Led by Party organs at various levels, they will experience the great storms of class struggle and two-line struggle so that they can raise their political awareness, enhance their talent, and mature through tempering. We must create even more favorable conditions to facilitate their involvement in the movement to learn from Tachai in agriculture. For this purpose, we must reduce the number of meetings which call for their participation outside of their brigades, provide more food for their political studies, and strive to rectify the ranks of poor and lower-middle peasants in places where the educated youths are stationed. We will spare no effort to justify the great expectations Chairman Mao and the Party have for us. During the great revolutionary movement for learning from Tachai in agriculture, we are determined to train the broad masses of educated youths to be reliable successors to the revolutionary cause of the proletariat.

With Class Struggle as the Key Link, Strive to Do a Good Job with Educated Youths

The CCP Committee of Hai-ch'eng
Hsien, Liaoning Province*

In an attempt to restore capitalism, the arch unrepentant capitalist-roader in the Party, Teng Hsiao-p'ing, dished up the revisionist program of "taking the three directives [of Mao] as the key link," advocating the theory that class struggle is dying out. Has class struggle died out? The answer is "no." The counterrevolutionary incident which took place at T'ien-an-men Square in April this year serves as new evidence in this connection. Through our work we are convinced that class struggle is ubiquitous and ever present. Only by taking class struggle as the key link can we expect to meet with success in all work.

Our great leader Chairman Mao instructed us that "educated youths must go to the villages," and "comrades from villages everywhere should welcome their going." Pursuant to his instruction, we have received more than fifty thousand resettled educated youths into our area since the Great Proletarian Cultural Revolution.

In what way can we do a good job in helping the educated youths who have gone up to the mountains and down to the countryside? At the beginning, we thought that all we could do

---

*Chung-kung Liao-ning sheng Hai-ch'eng hsien wei-yüan-hui, "I chieh-chi tou-cheng wei kang, tso hao chih-shih ch'ing-nien kung-tso." Jen-min jih-pao [People's Daily], May 5, 1976.

was to provide them with good food and lodgings and allow
them to do honest labor so that their parents could rest assured, and that would be enough. Therefore, we were more
concerned about their life and productive effort than about
other matters. In their efforts to cultivate a typical example
for youth points, comrades of the <u>hsien</u> office for resettling
educated youths invested several thousand <u>yuan</u> to build multi-
storied dwellings. They bought new window curtains and bed
sheets for the young people and helped set up a small factory
for them. They fully believed that this example would serve
very well. However, as things turned out, the youth point constantly ran into trouble and became a unit with "persistent,
great, and difficult problems." This was because we failed to
grasp class struggle as the key link and class enemies took advantage of the opportunity to stir up trouble. We encouraged
the educated youths to take root in the countryside to forge
revolution, while the enemies tried to poison the young people
with such absurd ideas as "one can become an official, if one
excels in studies," "study to become an official," and "farm
work is disguised reform through labor," preached by Confucius, Liu Shao-ch'i and Lin Piao, respectively. The enemies
resorted to all sorts of means to "uproot" the educated youths
from the countryside and undermine the drive to resettle the
young people there.

Facts have taught us that the overthrown landlord and capitalist classes will never take their defeat lying down. At no
time will they halt their efforts to revive the capitalist system, and they have all along vied desperately with us for successors. If we do not bear in mind the Party's basic line and
if we ignore the severe and complex class struggle in our work
with educated youths, we will be unable to take the initiative in
launching an offensive against the landlord and capitalist
classes. Consequently, we will fail in our work and certain
educated young people are liable to fall victim to the seduction
of the class enemy and degenerate into their tools for reviving
the capitalist system.

Having raised our understanding about this issue, we resolve to take class struggle as the key link persistently in our work among educated youths. By fully mobilizing the masses, we hit hard at the sabotage of a handful of class enemies.

The class enemy, as we have discovered, frequently spreads negative elements of feudalism, capitalism, and revisionism to corrupt the young people. For example, a bad person in Wang-t'ai Commune used to corrupt and poison the youths by offering them a smoke, a drink, a set of playing cards, or a pernicious book. We then mobilized the masses to reveal and criticize the bad person, which educated the young people deeply. The backward state in that youth point was quickly rectified.

Capitalist-roaders in the Party are in fact capitalists within the Party. By using and expanding the bourgeois rights, they oppose and wreck the movement to resettle the educated youths in the countryside. As they hold a degree of power in the Party, they are capable of exercising a role which class enemies should be in no position to play. If we do not wage a resolute struggle against the capitalists within the Party, we will suffer frustration and disruption in our work among the educated youths. Over the past few years, we have struck hard at bad people who have tried to sabotage the drive to resettle educated youths, especially those who persecute the young people.

In order to help educated young people raise their awareness of class struggle and two-line struggle so that they can take root in the countryside to forge revolution, we have set up political night schools and libraries in every youth point throughout the hsien. In addition, we have founded for them eight "communist universities" and a school for training, in rotation, backbone theorists from among the educated youths. We persistently organize the educated young people to study works of Marxism-Leninism and Chairman Mao and engage them in making constant criticism of the capitalist class and revisionism. Under the leadership of Party organizations at different levels, the educated youths actively participate in all kinds of political movements and conduct social surveys. They invite old poor peasants to speak to them about the history of the village and of the poor peasants' family life. All these endeavors have strengthened the educated youths' determination to take root in the countryside to carry on the revolution. New people and new deeds have emerged in great numbers. Many of them have voluntarily given up the opportunity to work in factories or to study at universities. They are determined to dedicate their youth to building a socialist new countryside.

Chairman Mao said: "The successors to the proletarian revolution are born from the masses, and grow up tempered by the great winds and waves of revolution." For the past several years we have regarded educated youths as a shock force in the movement to learn from Tachai in agriculture. We have allowed them to "face the world and brave the storm" [this refers to a saying of Mao in his article "Get Organized!" — Tr.] in the thick of class struggle, raised their consciousness of class struggle and line struggle, fully implementing their potential. Every year since 1974 we have chosen a batch of educated youths who had been well tempered to be transferred to backward teams where they were charged with the heavy task of reforming them. In Nan-t'ai Commune, Chu Ching-nan and eleven other educated youths were sent to work in a backward team. Led by the Party organization they relied on the strength of the poor and lower-middle peasants to grasp firmly the class struggle. They curbed such capitalist tendencies as expanding one's private plot and engaging in sideline occupations on one's own, and led the masses in a serious effort to learn from Tachai in agriculture. As a result of their endeavors, the team registered a dramatic increase in production from one hundred-odd chin per mou to more than 500, a yield which exceeded the target set in the National Agricultural Development Program. With the increase, the team has discarded the backward label of relying on the state for food supply, and effected a preliminary revamping of its backward look. We have made it a point to promote, in time, those outstanding educated young people to leading posts at various levels so that they can have access to more learning and tempering. Up to now, more than 1,200 young people from the educated youths in the entire hsien have joined the Chinese Communist Party. Over 17,000 educated youths have been admitted into the Communist Youth League and 424 young people have been appointed to be members of leading bodies at the commune and brigade levels. In addition, there are 3,860 youths serving in their respective communes and brigades as tutors for theoretical studies, agricultural technicians, tractor drivers, teachers of primary schools run by the collective, barefoot doctors, and so forth. The broad masses of educated youths are now sturdily maturing in the Three Great Revolutionary Movements in the rural areas.

In retrospect, we know that the reason we were able to score certain achievements in our work was that we had placed a great emphasis on grasping class struggle as the key link. We must make deep and penetrating criticism of Teng Hsiao-p'ing's revisionist program of "taking the three directives as the key link" and counterattack the right-deviationist tendency to reverse the correct verdict. We must persist in taking class struggle as the key link and adhere to the Party's basic line, striving to train and cultivate millions of successors to the revolutionary cause of the proletariat.

Glossary

"Back door" [hou-men 后門]

> Using influence to achieve special interests rather than following standard procedures.

"Bourgeois right" [tzu-ch'an chieh-chi fa-ch'üan 资产阶级法权]

> Refers to the class privileges of the bourgeoisie in capitalist society and to attitudes of those in socialist society who would use influence and position to achieve special interests. An example would be cadres using their influence to send their children to university through the "back door," q.v.

Brigade [ta tui 大队]

> Second of three administrative levels in a rural commune. Coordinates the activities of several production teams, q.v. The size of brigades varies greatly in different locations, but they average about 200-300 households.

Cadre [kan-pu 干部]

> One who holds an official leadership position in Party, army, government or mass organization.

Ching-kang-shan [井冈山]

In Kiangsi Province — one of the earliest rural bases of the Communists.

Chin [斤]

Measurement of weight: about $1\frac{1}{3}$ pounds.

"Cold palace" [leng kung 冷宫]

Refers to the banishing of former imperial favorites in traditional China.

Commune [kung-she 公社]

Lowest level of state government. Highest of three administrative levels of collective ownership and production in rural areas — the others being brigades and production teams, q.v.

"Counterrevolutionary incident at T'ien-an-men Square" (April 1976) [T'ien-an men kuang-ch'ang ti fan ko-ming cheng-chih shih-chien 天安门广场的反革命政治事件]

A demonstration of support for Teng Hsiao-p'ing and the policies of Chou En-lai on April 5, 1976, in reaction to the removal of flowers from a memorial to Chou En-lai. At the time, the press said the incident had been planned by Teng Hsiao-p'ing in a move to seize power. Teng was immediately dismissed from all posts. Since the fall of the "Gang of Four" (Chiang-Ch'ing, Chang Ch'un-ch'iao, Wang Hung-wen and Yao Wen-yuan), the incident has been blamed on them as part of a plot to get rid of Teng and discredit Chou. Teng has since been exonerated.

"Cross the Yellow River" [k'ua-kuo Huang-ho 跨过黄河]

Producing more than 200 kilograms per mou, q.v., the

target set for areas north of the Yellow River by the National Program for Agricultural Development.

Educated youths [chih-shih ch'ing-nien 知 识 青 年]

Refers to youths educated at least through junior middle-school (grade 7).

"Force (ourselves) across the Yangtze River" [ch'iang tu Ch'ang chiang 强 渡 长 江]

To produce more than 400 kilograms per mou, q.v., the target set for areas south of the Yangtze River by the National Program for Agricultural Development.

Hsia-fang cadre [hsia-fang kan-pu 下 放 干 部]

Cadres, q.v., who have been sent down to lower level administrative posts, often in rural areas, during drive for decentralization, economizing, improvement of rural areas and/or cadre reform. Hsia-fang can be either temporary or permanent.

Hsien [县]

A district. The administrative level above communes; sometimes translated "county."

K'ang [炕]

A brick bed warmed by a fire, used in North China.

K'ang-ta [抗 大]

The Communists' foremost cadre training institution in the early years of the Yenan period, q.v. During the Cultural Revolution it was publicized as a model for Chairman Mao's educational ideas.

Kuomintang [Kuo-min-tang 国 民 党]

The Nationalist Party organized by Sun Yat-sen in 1912,

and reorganized by Sun with the help of the Comintern in 1923. It led the government of China from 1927 to 1949 when its leaders were defeated by the Communists and fled to Taiwan where they are still in control.

"Learn from Tachai in Agriculture" [Nung-yeh hsüeh Ta-chai 农业学大寨]

Once poor and unable to support itself, Tachai Brigade, under the leadership of Ch'en Yun-kuei, became a national model for self-reliance, persistance and hard work.

li [里]

A measure of distance: about $\frac{1}{3}$ of a mile (more exactly, 1,890 feet).

Lin Piao [林彪] (1907-1971)

Minister of National Defense and de facto head of the Military Affairs Committee of the Communist Party. Officially named Mao Tse-tung's successor by the Party Constitution at the Ninth Party Congree in 1969. Plotted to overthrow Mao in 1971 and was killed in a plane crash trying to escape when the plot was discovered. In a subsequent campaign to criticize Lin and Confucius he was denigrated as a self-seeking careerist and an elitist who despised the masses.

Liu Shao-ch'i [刘少奇]

Communist Party Politburo member from 1927 to 1968. Chairman of the Government and of the National Defense Council of the People's Republic of China from 1959 to 1968. Attacked during the Great Proletarian Cultural Revolution as the "principal person in authority taking the capitalist road." Dismissed from all posts and from the Party.

"Long March" [ch'ang-cheng 长征]

The Communists' trek from the Kiangsi Soviet in central China to the Northwest in 1934-35. Today it symbolizes dedication and courage to overcome all obstacles.

Lu Hsün [鲁迅]

Pseudonym of Chou Shu-jen (1881-1936). Prominent writer and social critic, greatly admired by Mao Tse-tung and held up as a model for revolutionary writers.

"May 7" (Evening School) [wu ch'i 五.七]

Refers to Chairman Mao's directive of May 7, 1966, in which he called on students and others to "learn other things" including industrial production, agriculture, and military affairs while mainly engaging in academics or their regular work.

mou [亩]

Land measure: 6.6 mou equal one acre.

"One strike, 2 Anti movement" [i-ta san-fan yun-tung 一打三反运动]

Campaign in 1969 to strike counterrevolutionaries and oppose corruption and theft, speculation, waste and extravagance.

Poor and lower-middle peasants [p'in hsia-chung nung 贫下中农]

Peasants who, before collectivization, were either barely able to produce enough on their own land to sustain themselves (lower-middle), or were unable to and had to rent land (poor).

"Red and expert" [yu hung, yu chuan 又红又专]

Both ideologically correct and vocationally competent.

"Taking three directives of Chairman Mao as the key link"
[san hsiang chih-shih wei kang 三項指示为纲]

> Criticism of Teng Hsiao-p'ing after his dismissal from all posts in April 1976. He is said to have tried to subvert Chairman Mao's emphasis on "class struggle as the key link" by giving equal weight to Chairman Mao's instructions to promote stability and unity, push the national economy forward, and study the theory of proletarian dictatorship and combat and prevent revisionsim.

Teng Hsiao-p'ing [邓小平]

> High Party and government official, criticized during the Cultural Revolution as the "number two person in authority taking the revisionist road; dismissed from all posts. Reinstated as vice premier by Chou En-lai in 1975. Dismissed again after the "counterrevolutionary incident of T'ien-an-men Square," q.v., April 1976. Rehabilitated after the fall of the "Gang of Four" in late 1976.

"Three great differences" [san ta fen-pieh 三大分别]

> Between city and countryside, mental and manual labor, workers and peasants.

Three Great Revolutionary Movements (in the countryside)
[san ta ko-ming yun-tung 三大革命运动]

> Class struggle, production struggle, scientific experimentation

"Three histories" [san shih 三史]

> In 1964 peasants were urged to recall the bitterness of the past and record it in the "three histories": personal,

family and village. This was part of a movement to reform cadres and promote class struggle. It was one of
a number of measures preliminary to the Great Proletarian Cultural Revolution.

"Three-in-one" (management) [san chieh-ho 三 结 合]

Refers to the formation of a representative group. Ideally
such a group would consist of a broad spectrum of ages,
interests and talents.

"Three levels" [san chi 三 级]

The three administrative levels on a rural commune —
commune, brigade, production team, q.v.

"Up to the mountains, down to the countryside" [shang shan
hsia hsiang 上 山 下 乡]

A term first used in 1968 referring to the program to
resettle educated urban youths in the countryside.

Work team, or production team [kung-tso tui 工 作 队]

The lowest of three administrative levels in a rural
commune. Teams vary in size, but average about 40
households.

Yenan [Yen-an 延 安]

A city in Shensi Province. The headquarters of the
Chinese Communist Movement from 1937 to 1947.

Youth points [ch'ing-nien tien 青 年 点]

Places where resettled urban youths live together in a
rural commune.

Yuan [园]

Unit of currency: worth approximately U.S. $.50.

About the Contributors

A graduate of the University of Cincinnati, Peter J. Seybolt received a Ph.D. in History and Far Eastern Languages from Harvard University in 1970. He is an associate professor of history at the University of Vermont.

Dr. Seybolt has published numerous articles and translations in various journals and is the editor of the books Revolutionary Education in China: Documents and Commentary (1973), Through Chinese Eyes (1974), and, with Gregory Chiang, Language Reform in China (forthcoming). He is also the editor of the journal Chinese Education.

A graduate of Harvard College, Thomas P. Bernstein received an M.A., a Certificate from the Russian Institute, and a Ph.D. (in 1970) from Columbia University. He has taught at Indiana University and Yale University, and he is now an associate professor of political science at Columbia University.

Dr. Bernstein has published numerous articles and reviews on China and comparative communism and is the author of Up to the Mountains and Down to the Villages: The Transfer of Youth from Urban to Rural China (1977). He is currently at work on a comparative study of the collectivization of agriculture in Russia and China.